STUFF YOUNG ADULTS SHOULD KNOW

Essential Life Skills, Tips, and Advice to Thrive as an Adult!

JAKE RUSSELL

ISBN: 978-1-957590-43-1

For questions, email: Support@AwesomeReads.org

Please consider writing a review!

Just visit: AwesomeReads.org/review

FREE BONUS

SCAN TO GET OUR NEXT BOOK FOR FREE!

TABLE OF CONTENTS

INTRODUCTION

So, you've decided to go live by yourself and start your independent journey. First of all, congratulations. I am proud of your decision—welcome to adulthood.

Let's be honest, this transition is going to be overwhelming at first, as all big transitions are. There are lots of things to learn, and while you can always ask for help from your parents or hire someone to do things for you, it's a really good idea to know how to do most things yourself. Having a basic knowledge of day-to-day challenges you might encounter and how to resolve them will definitely come in handy.

The advantages of being self-reliant are numerous, starting with the fact that it will help you save money. Especially if you just decided to get your own place, you will be faced with a lot of expenses. Being able to take care of some jobs on your own, without having to hire others to do those jobs for you, will be a great source of savings. Coasting through life without knowing how to do the most basic things or understanding how things work can be extremely challenging, and you don't need that extra hardship on your plate.

Yes, some parts of it are serious, but this phase of life is also going to be extremely exciting!

You will be gaining more and more confidence in yourself and your abilities as you move forward to conquer some independent milestones in your adult life.

Having some solid skills will be essential to help you meet and overcome all the challenges of everyday life you will inevitably face. In addition, these life skills bring both mental and physical benefits to the individual person, such as problem-solving abilities, being able to analyze the options in each situation and make better decisions, and developing a greater sense of self-awareness.

In this book, we will cover the main life skills you should start to familiarize yourself with at this stage of your life. We'll cover everything from physical knowledge to how to fix a drywall hole in your new apartment!

CHAPTER ONE:
TAKING CARE
OF YOURSELF

First, we're going to start by getting to know more about how to take care of our bodies and our health, because if we are unhealthy or sick, we won't get very far.

GET TO KNOW THE HEALTH CARE SYSTEM

First, you will need to get acquainted with the type of health care system that's available in your country. Countries around the world have different types of health care systems. You'll want to start out by understanding the four major models that are used:

The Beveridge Model: In this model, the government is the sole payer, therefore the national health service is in control of prices. This type of health care system is funded through taxpayer money, and there are no out-of-pocket expenses for patients or any co-sharing costs. Each taxpaying citizen is ensured the same access to health care. This type of model can be found in the following countries, among others: the United Kingdom, Italy, Spain, Denmark, Sweden, Norway, and New Zealand. With this type of health care model, you will never receive a bill for your trips to the doctor or the hospital.

The Bismarck Model: Unlike the Beveridge model, this type of health care system does not provide a universal health coverage. To have access to health care, one is required to be employed, and either the employer or the employee is responsible for funding their health insurance through payroll deductions. In this model, the providers and hospitals are generally private but the insurers are public. Some countries have only one insurance company (e.g., France), while in other countries (e.g., Germany) you might have a wider option of insurance companies. This type of model can be found in the Netherlands, Japan, and Switzerland, among other countries.

The National Health Insurance Model: This system is a combination of both the Beveridge and Bismarck models. This type of health care system uses private providers who are paid through insurance programs that are run by the government. There is a balance between private and public sector, which encourages cheaper prices. This type of model is used in Canada, Taiwan, and South Korea.

The Out-of-Pocket Model: This model is extremely common in countries that have a smaller governmental infrastructure. Since these smaller infrastructures are often limited by a lack of funds or resources, it is difficult to create a medical system. So, in this type of model, the patient is in charge of all the expenses.

Mixed Systems: A clear example of a mixed system is the health care system in the United States, where there is no universal coverage provided. Mixed systems use both public-financed government health care and health care provided through private organizations.

CHOOSING A DOCTOR

If you are feeling unwell or aware of some sort of discomfort in your body, you'll want to identify the correct person with whom to discuss your concerns. There are many different types of health-care providers, all with their own specialties. Here is a list of some types of doctors you may commonly encounter:

Allergists are specialized in the field of allergies. If you suffer from disorders such as asthma, eczema, food allergies, or insect allergies, this will likely be the doctor for your case.

Dermatologists are specialized in the field of skin-related disorders, such as acne, moles, scars, skin allergies, and more.

Physiatrists are specialized in the rehabilitation of neck and back pain caused by injuries, accidents, or diseases.

Podiatrists specialize in problems related to the feet and ankles.

Obstetricians and/or Gynecologists, also known as OB/GYNs, specialize in care for women and the female reproductive organs, including pregnancy and childbirth.

Optometrists are specialized in eye testing and prescribing medications related to eye conditions, such as correct eyeglasses.

Dentists specialize in the care of the teeth and gums.

To visit a specialist like those listed above, you may need to first visit your **primary care physician (PCP)**, who will give you a referral. Your PCP is the primary, general doctor you see for annual physicals, general medical questions, or whenever you're not sure who to talk to about a health concern. In most cases, you'll need to get that referral from your PCP in order to see a specialist. So, when in doubt, ask your primary care physician.

COMMON ILLNESSES AND HOME TREATMENTS

It's easy to get scared and imagine the worst when we feel sick or worry that we are injured. But in fact, it's not always necessary to rush to the doctor at the first sign of illness. Here are some diseases and their symptoms that can be easily treated at home.

ALLERGIES

If you already know that you have allergies—perhaps you were diagnosed as a child—then you may be able to treat your symptoms effectively at home. Common triggers for allergies can be:

Food (nuts, eggs, milk, soy, shellfish, etc.), with symptoms including skin rashes, diarrhea, nausea, vomiting, excessive gas, swelling, and difficulty breathing.

Environmental allergens like pollen, pet hair, or mold, all of which share similar symptoms including eye irritation, runny nose, sneezing, stuffy nose, puffy and red eyes, sneezing, itchy nose and throat, etc.

You may have already been prescribed medications for your allergies, if needed. Remember that for mild allergies, your best bet is to avoid the allergen whenever you can. But if your symptoms are not manageable, or you are not able to fully avoid the allergen, then one of the over-the-counter medications below may help. Always talk with your primary care physician before you begin treating yourself for allergies. Allergy medications can be divided into three major groups:

Antihistamines: prevent itchiness, sneezing, hives.

Decongestants: help clear your airways (nose and mouth) by narrowing the blood vessels that supply the membranes in your nose and mouth.

Anti-inflammatory agents: help to reduce swelling of your respiratory tracts.

COLD AND FLU

The flu—also known as influenza—and colds are the most common type of illnesses. Both the flu and the common cold attack your respiratory tract and may lead to a fever, as your body raises its temperature in an attempt to kill the virus or bacteria that is making you sick. If you have a high fever or suspect you have the flu, contact your doctor. If you seem to have just a mild cold, here are some common at-home treatments that can help to alleviate your symptoms:

- Rest as much as possible.
- Drink a lot of non-alcoholic, non-caffeinated fluids— your goal is to keep yourself well-hydrated.
- Honey and lemon can be useful to relieve a sore throat.
- Tea infused with ginger sometimes helps to relieve feelings of nausea.

CONJUNCTIVITIS:

Conjunctivitis is an inflammation of the transparent membrane of your eyelids and eyeballs. The causes may vary, including infection, allergic reaction, or irritation caused by an external agent. If you have conjunctivitis, your eyes might appear red, you may feel itchiness and a sensation of burning in your eyes, and you may have pus discharge and crusting on your eyelids. Some of the most common treatments are to:

- Avoid rubbing your eyes.

- Soak any crusting with a cool, wet, and clean cloth.
- Do not use any type of makeup until your symptoms have fully resolved.
- Over-the-counter eye drops can help relieve the itchiness (ask your doctor or the pharmacist for a recommendation so that you don't inadvertently worsen your condition).
- Do not wear any contact lenses until symptoms are healed.

If your physical condition worsens, visit your primary care physician.

DIARRHEA AND UPSET STOMACH

This type of discomfort can be caused by several different factors, such as bacterial infections, parasites, food intolerance, or eating food that has gone bad or that has not been cooked properly. Common treatments can be as easy as to:

- Avoid food or liquids that will require your body more strength to process.
- Avoid caffeine, which will cause dehydration.
- Avoid high sugar drinks.
- Use over-the-counter medicines such as Imodium.
- Consume probiotics that can be found in food such as dark chocolate, green olives, and yogurt.
- Eat low-fiber food such as bananas and rice.

HEADACHES

Causes of headache can vary widely and can be related to your body or to your mental state. For example, common causes of headache include stress, fatigue, irregular sleeping habits, excessive intake of caffeine, alcohol, and medicine side effects. Some of the most common treatments are:

- A healthy amount of sleep on a consistent schedule.
- Consuming sufficient water and liquids to ensure adequate hydration.
- Use of over-the-counter medicines such as ibuprofen, acetaminophen, or aspirin.
- An ice pack held over the eyes or forehead can provide short-term relief.

If you have long-lasting, frequent, or severe headaches, contact your primary care physician.

USEFUL MEDICINES TO KEEP ON HAND

Medicines are best taken if prescribed by your primary care physician. But there are some over-the-counter medicines that are good to keep around in your house to treat minor illnesses, such as colds or headaches.

Acetaminophen, Aspirin, Ibuprofen, or Naproxen: pain relivers and fever reducers. These medications can be used to reduce inflammation like that which may accompany a toothache. They are generally used when you have a fever or some sort of pain in your body. Consult your doctor to determine which of these pain-reliever options is best for you, and make sure to keep some on hand.

Antihistamine: to use when you are having an allergic reaction such as itchiness or hives.

Decongestants, most commonly known as cough syrup: to use for congestion, like a runny nose or cough.

Antacids: to use if you are experiencing heartburn or acid reflux.

Bandages (e.g., BandAids): to use if you accidentally cut yourself. Bandages help to stop bleeding, allow the wound to heal, and also help to keep the area clean during that process.

Thermometer: to check your temperature if you are not feeling well. You'll want to know whether you have a fever and to monitor your temperature in case you need to see the doctor. Normal body temperature is 37°C, or 98.6°F. You should immediately call a doctor if your temperature goes higher than 39.4°C, or 103°F.

Disinfectant and alcohol wipes: to clean a wound, helping to prevent infections around the injured area.

Calamine lotion: to use on your skin if you have a rash.

Antidiarrheal: to use if you are having problems with an irritated bowel. This will help your gut slow down the movement and will decrease your stool.

Sunscreen: for use throughout the year. Even on winter days, it's important to protect your skin from UV radiation that can be harmful in the long run.

EMERGENCY KITS

You should have an emergency kit ready at all times that will keep you safe and help you in emergency situations. Many drugstores or other stores offer pre-stocked emergency kits. If you prefer to make your own emergency or first aid kit, here are some things you should include:

Bandages in various sizes and shapes. These will help you control bleeding caused by minor injuries, and will also help your wounded area avoid infection while it heals.

Sterile gauze dressing in various sizes. Gauze can be used in several ways to protect and clean a wound. It can be used as a temporary absorbent over the wounded area, and if sterilized it can be used to clean the wounded area.

Safety pins. These can be used to hold together and secure bandages that have been placed over a wounded area.

Disposable sterile gloves. These are very important in case you need to treat a wound. Using sterile gloves will protect you from any bacteria or contact with another person's blood, and they also protect the wound from infection.

Scissors. You might think scissors aren't necessary, but if you ever find yourself in a situation where you have to cut through someone clothes in order to perform first aid, having a pair of scissors will cut the time in half, and will also help if you find yourself needing to go through multiple layers of clothing. They are also useful for cutting bandages so that they can be kept cleaned and sterilized, avoiding contact with other highly bacterial transmissive tools.

Alcohol-free cleansing wipes. These can be used to safely clean the skin around a wound from blood or dirt.

Sticky tape to attach bandages and gauzes.

Thermometer to detect someone's temperature.

Antiseptic cream. Apply it to the wounded area to protect against possible infections.

Distilled water to wash a wound in order to clean it.

FLU SEASON

Have you ever asked yourself why a certain period of the year is also commonly called the flu season? This term is generally used to denote a specific time frame within the year when contagion for illness like the flu tends to be higher. Flu season normally coincides with the months that mark cold weather. In the Northern Hemisphere, for example, this typically means roughly October through March, which are generally the coldest months of the year. Of course, depending on one's location in the world this time frame will change. For example, in Australia cold weather comes during the months from June to August, which is the winter period there.

What is the best way to be prepared for this season? The best thing you can do to protect yourself from the seasonal flu is to get your seasonal flu shot. Other steps can be taken to avoid getting sick during the coldest months, such as:

Avoiding close contact with people who are sick.

Staying home when you are sick, to reduce the chances of spreading the flu to the people you have contact with on a daily basis. As obvious as this may seem, many people don't realize how much of a domino effect the flu can have. One person who is sick can infect many other people, who will go on to infect other people as well.

Wash your hands frequently throughout the day. This practice will protect you and others from germs that are on your hands.

When you have to cough or sneeze, cover your mouth and nose. Besides being good manners, this will also prevent airborne viruses and bacteria from spreading through saliva particles.

Clean all of the surfaces in your house that you touch often — like counters, tables, and doorknobs — using disinfecting wipes.

Eat healthy food to boost your immune system.

Get plenty of rest and sleep to keep your immune system strong.

A POST COVID-19 WORLD

Since the beginning of the Covid-19 pandemic, we have all learned about the extra steps we should be taking to avoid getting infected. While the presence of a vaccine has made the situation less alarming, it is still a good practice to practice hygiene and safety so that we can avoid accidentally infecting others.

If you are feeling mild symptoms that can be associated with the coronavirus, stay at home and avoid travelling.

Where possible, practice social distancing. The CDC recommends keeping a six-foot distance between yourself and others.

Keep your hands clean even more than you usually do. In addition to washing your hands with soap, you may want to use hand sanitizers that are at least 60% alcohol as well.

Clean your household surfaces on a daily basis with disinfectants.

Last but not least, if you have contracted the virus, do not panic. There are available treatments and doctors will help you and make sure you are back on your feet in no time. Remember that this disease is not unknown to us anymore. Call your primary care doctor so you can be guided and properly walked through the next steps that you will be taking.

If you do think you are experiencing an emergency, call your regional emergency number. Here are some helpful international emergency numbers:

- Europe: 112
- South Africa: 10
- India: 100 or 112
- South Korea: 02-112
- China: 119
- Japan: 110
- North America: 911
- Western Sahara: 150
- Thailand: 191

Some countries have local numbers only. These numbers can be easily found on the internet; simply type a few keywords such as "emergency number + your location."

CHAPTER TWO:
WHAT YOU EAT MATTERS

VITAMINS

Most important vitamins and minerals that we need can be found in the food we eat daily. However, sometimes we find that our lives are especially busy and we aren't eating as healthfully as we would like. If this occurs regularly, supplements could help to ensure you are taking in proper nutrition. Talk with your doctor before beginning any supplement regimen.

Here is a list of supplements you might keep in your home that could help you with your health.

Vitamin D is extremely important for the health of our bones. It helps our nervous system in sending messages from our brain to the rest of our body, and it helps fight bacteria and viruses. A lack of vitamin D can cause various health issues and has even been associated with depression.

Probiotics are important for our digestive system. Probiotics are also known as good bacteria that help boost our immune system and reduce inflammations and allergies.

Vitamin C also helps boost our immune system. It assists in the production of white blood cells which are helpful to fight infections.

Zinc helps to heal damaged tissues (for example a wound), helps our immune system, and encourages the growth of cells.

Vitamins of the B group play a major role in the maintenance of our health. Vitamin B can influence our energy, the function of our brain, and the metabolism of our cells.

Magnesium can help in regulating blood sugar levels and blood pressure. It improves the health of our bones, and helps the well-being of our heart.

Melatonin is a hormone that is normally produced by our body. Sometimes we might find ourselves in need of supplements of melatonin because our body is not producing a sufficient quantity, which can cause trouble sleeping.

GET TO KNOW YOUR KITCHEN

Cooking can be difficult—maybe you're not a big fan of the kitchen, it's the first time you're trying to cook something from scratch, or maybe it's the first time you're buying kitchen tools. The best way to make this process easier for you is become familiar with the most common tools you should have in your kitchen.

Knives. Make sure you always have a proper knife that will cut through your food without you needing to struggle too much. A good knife is a knife that has a sharp blade and a good handle for a better grip; you don't want to accidentally cut yourself while you're trying to make yourself a meal.

Knife sharpener. Even the best knives start to become dull with time. A knife sharpener will allow you to sharpen even the most stubborn of knives.

Cutting board. You'll want to have at least two cutting boards in your home. One should be used only for raw meat and the other for cooked food or produce. This way, you'll avoid contamination from raw meat, which can carry bacteria until it is properly cooked.

Mixing bowls. While the material doesn't matter, having at least two mixing bowls will save you a lot of time when you're trying to prepare a meal.

Cookware. You obviously can't cook if you don't have pans. There are various types of pans according to their function. The most common types are:

- **Cast iron skillets** can be used to cook most kinds of foods and typically can be used on the stovetop as well as inside the oven.
- **Frying pans** can be used on the stovetop to cook many different kinds of foods using a variety of techniques, including searing, frying, and sauteeing.
- **Saucepans** hold a greater volume of liquid, so they're perfect when you're cooking a sauce, boiling water, or heating up something like a soup or stew.
- **Stockpots** are larger saucepans and are often used for very large quantities, like making soup for a crowd or boiling a whole chicken to make chicken stock.

Utensils that will be helpful in your meal preparation may include:

- **Wooden spoons** come in handy as they don't scratch pans and don't get too hot even when they're left in a hot pot.
- **A peeler** will make peeling your fruits and vegetables much faster. You can also use a small knife for this purpose, but a peeler will be easier.
- **Whisks** help you emulsify liquid ingredients such as oil, vinegar, egg whites, and more.
- **Tongs** are used to flip food, like meat or fish, while it's cooking in a pan.

Storage containers, so you can store your leftovers properly in your fridge.

BASIC SEASONINGS TO KEEP ON HAND

Almost all recipes call for the inclusion of seasonings. While you may need other seasonings for your favorite meals, here's a list of some of the most common seasonings you may want to keep on hand:

Cinnamon, which can be used in both sweet and savory dishes.

Paprika. You can experiment to determine the kind you like best, as there are sweet paprikas, smoked paprikas, and more.

Black pepper, a seasoning commonly used in most savory dishes.

Onion powder can help enhance flavor while adding a subtle sweetness to the dish.

Garlic powder, used similarly to onions.

Dried herbs such as basil, rosemary, cilantro, oregano, and parsley will be useful in numerous recipes.

Ginger, besides being a very good ally to your health, can add a pungent, spicy, and sweet taste to a dish.

Curry powder. This type of spice, like paprika, has different tastes. You can choose a sweet type of curry or find a spicy one.

Nutmeg adds some warmth and depth to your dish.

Last but not least—salt. Salt is the most basic universal seasoning that is used to add flavor to a dish.

TYPES OF OILS

There are several types of oil that can be used when cooking, and it's a good idea to familiarize yourself with the options.

Unless otherwise noted, all of these oils should be stored in a cool, dark place, not in the fridge.

Extra-virgin olive oil. This is probably one of the most well-known oils. This type of oil is very healthy and can be used to cook most food. It can also be used as a condiment, such as in salad dressings. It's best to remember that this type of oil should not be used for frying—in fact, once cooked above 375°F (191°C) it loses its beneficial properties.

Light olive oil. This type of olive oil, unlike extra-virgin olive oil, can be used for higher temperature of cooking. For example, to grill, roast or to sauté your veggies.

Coconut oil. This is often used outside the kitchen as a treatment for hair and skin. But when used for cooking, this type of oil is ideal when making meals that require a higher temperature, for example when frying.

Vegetable and canola oils. These types of oil are perfect for grilling, frying, stir-frying, and baking meals that require a high temperature.

Avocado oil. Avocado is well known to be a very healthy supplement for our heart with its healthy, unsaturated fats. This type of oil is perfect for frying, roasting, and grilling, because of its capability of enduring extremely high temperatures. Avocado oil can be stored in a cool, dark place, and it can be also be stored in the fridge.

Peanut oil. This type of oil is best used as a dressing or to add flavor to your dishes.

To recap:

The types of oils that are recommended for frying are: canola oil, vegetable oil, avocado oil, and coconut oil.

Types of oils for a lower-medium temperature: extra-virgin olive oil, light olive oil.

Types of oils that are good to be used as seasoning: extra-virgin olive oil, light olive oil, and peanut oil.

HEALTHY REPLACEMENTS

Maintaining a good balance with your food intake is the key to staying healthy and avoiding extra trips to the doctor. If you are a big fan of junk food, know that there are lots of ways to replace those unhealthy foods with things that your body will thank you for later in your life. So, whether you are a big junk food lover or not, here's a list of some quick and delicious healthy replacements.

Replace granola with nuts. As harmless and easy as it might seem, granola is always loaded with extra sugar. If you don't want to miss that crunch, you can substitute nuts instead.

Replace mayo with chickpea-based hummus. If you are a big fan of mayo on your sandwiches, consider replacing it with chickpea-based hummus.

You can replace your beloved chips with veggies. For example, you can cut a zucchini into small round slices, sprinkle them with some salt and drizzle with some oil, put them in the oven and take them out once they are golden.

Trade your potato chips for some kale chips: remove the ribs of the kale, and then cut it into the desired pieces. Sprinkle some salt on top and drizzle some oil, then place them in the oven until crisp.

Did you know you can replace your conventional pasta with spaghetti squash? First, cut a spaghetti squash in half and place it in the oven. Once the skin turns golden, take your squash out of the oven and let it cool. Once cool, grab a fork and start scraping the inside of the vegetable. Strands will form that are very similar to spaghetti, and you can use whatever sauce you like!

Replace your rice with riced cauliflower. All you need is a cheese grater and a strong arm. Grate your cauliflower until completely finished. You will end up with a healthy substitute for rice.

Replace packaged cereal with oatmeal. Packaged cereals are always very tempting — first, because the packages are made to catch our attention and second, because they are obviously delicious. But a good substitute for cereal is oatmeal. Not only is it healthier, but you can top it with anything you wish!

Replace mayo with Greek yogurt. Another replacement for mayonnaise is Greek yogurt. The texture is very similar, and it is far healthier than mayonnaise.

Substitute cauliflower for potatoes. Potatoes are good in moderation, but they can be heavy for your stomach. So substituting them every now and then with cauliflower might be a good idea for a healthier diet.

Replace wheat flour with coconut flour. Coconut flower can be a valid and healthy substitute as it is rich in fiber and has more protein. It can be used for baking everything from cakes to bread, and it will add that hint of coconut that coconut lovers are going to enjoy!

Sugar is not healthy when consumed in excessive amounts, so consider Stevia as a substitute. Stevia is plant based and can be used in all sorts of drinks that you normally like to sweeten, such as coffee.

GETTING TO KNOW WHAT'S IN SEASON

Most of the time grocery stores have all we need, if not even more. It's often easy to find even fruits and vegetables that are out of season. But sometimes, opting for an out of season fruit or vegetable can be a bad idea. First of all, they're not as fresh as they seem. Out of season fruits and vegetables are often picked underripe and then preserved, which removes a lot of the health benefits you expect from this food. Out of season produce also tastes less flavorful than they normally would. Out of season fruits and vegetables, no matter where you are in the world, have either been imported or grown in heated or custom-made greenhouses, so they're often more expensive than seasonal fruits and vegetables. Knowing which fruits or vegetables are grown in each season can be beneficial to your health and to your wallet.

Summer

- Berries: although they can be found throughout the whole year, summer is considered to be berries' peak season.
- Cherries
- Squash: zucchini and yellow squash are extremely versatile when it comes to meal prep.
- Corn, garlic, eggplant, and cucumber.
- Cantaloupe and other melons.
- Stone fruits: peaches, apricots, nectarines, and plums.
- All types of tomatoes.
- Watermelon.
- Grapes' peak season is usually toward the end of the summer, a sweet way to end the hot days of the year.

Fall

- Apples
- Bananas
- Broccoli
- Bell Peppers

- Grapes
- Mushrooms
- Kale
- Potatoes
- Pears
- Spinach
- Onions
- Lettuce
- Kiwi
- Olives
- Persimmons

Winter

- Chestnuts
- Turnips
- Lemons
- Radishes
- Citrons
- Kiwi
- Limes
- Olives
- Pomegranates

Spring

- Apples

- Cabbage
- Broccoli
- Carrots
- Celery
- Lettuce
- Radishes
- Spinach
- Asparagus
- Avocados
- Apricots
- Collard greens

CHOOSING HEALTHY GROCERIES

Grocery shopping can be overwhelming, especially because of the infinite number of products to choose from. Getting lost and buying things you don't actually need is extremely easy, especially if you don't have a grocery list. It's a very common mistake to be seduced by appealing products. A lot of people end up either buying things they don't need or buying food that is about to go bad. Knowing how to choose your groceries the right way can save your wallet.

First and foremost, before heading to the store make sure to check your fridge and your pantry. Make a list of the things you need that you eat regularly. This way you can avoid buying things you'll only end up throwing away.

Buy perishable food in quantities you know for a fact you will use. If you are not sure, opt for a lower quantity — you can always make an extra trip or buy more on the next trip to the store. This way you will avoid tossing spoiled food in the garbage.

Buy fresh, seasonal fruits and vegetables. If you buy too much, you can always freeze your perishable goods for later use rather than wasting them.

If you are living by yourself, check the portions on the packages you buy. This will help you plan your meals better.

When buying fresh produce, you should always follow the three golden rules:

Look

Check that the vegetable or the fruit is the appropriate color, without brown spots or wilted edges. If you are planning on eating the fresh produce later in the week, opt for something that is not completely ripe yet, which will allow you to avoid eating overly ripe food at the end of the week. For example, if you are buying some bananas and hope they will last several days, go for the ones that have not completely turned yellow yet and are still green. This means that they're not completely ripe yet and will still need a day or two to be ready.

Smell

Fruits normally smell slightly sweet. If they don't have a sweet scent, this means that they're not quite ripe. On the other hand, a strong, fruity, sweet scent means that the fruit is overripe and will probably go bad soon.

Touch

Touching the fresh produce you are about to buy can help you determine its ripeness. For example, leafy greens should be green and not soft. Berries should be soft but not mushy. Stone fruits, such as peaches, should be firm but not hard — hardness means that they are far from being ripe. When it comes to melons, the heavier they are the juicier they will be.

Knowing the differences between types of grocery stores can help you find the perfect store for your needs.

Supermarkets

Supermarkets are chain stores that normally include daily living products such as food, toiletries, house maintenance products, cleaning detergents, clothing, and more. They carry a wide variety of products and may be likely to have everything you need, great for when you want to finish your whole list at once.

Wholesale Stores

This type of store normally sells products in bulk, which is especially handy if you have a large family. The unit prices in these stores are usually lower than supermarkets, and they usually require an annual membership fee.

Natural Food Stores

This type of store normally has organic foods and their selection most likely includes local products. The produce in natural food stores is typically fresher than in supermarkets.

Discount Stores

These stores normally sell items that other stores do not sell, perhaps because the package shows slight damage or the expiration date has recently passed.

Always check the expiration date. It can happen that from time to time, stores sell expired products. This can be unpleasant, especially for dairy products. You'll want to avoid buying food that is too close to the expiration date, to avoid useless waste.

ALL ABOUT ORGANIC, GMO, AND PLANT-BASED FOODS

Organic Food

When food is marked as organic, it refers to the way that food is first grown and then processed. Organic food is grown without using external agents, such as pesticides, fertilizers, artificial flavors, colors, or preservatives.

GMO

GMO stands for "Genetically Modified Organisms." As sci-fi as this sounds, it's not as scary or wild as it seems — at least, not all the time. Common GMOs include apples, watermelons, bananas, corn, and potatoes. Without genetic modification, apples would still be tart and only useful for alcoholic ciders. Bananas and watermelon used to have very little fruit — banana seeds were large and watermelon had six sections that were mostly inedible rind. Corn was nothing more than a thin blade of wheat-like grain before modification birthed the modern ear. All of these plants have been genetically modified over the course of thousands of years through selective growing and breeding practices.

In the modern era, however, biotechnology has allowed scientists to alter organisms more quickly and in a more direct manner. By editing the DNA rather than slowly breeding select plants, food can be altered for purposes such as having a longer shelf life or withstanding pesticides. These newer practices and alterations are what have given GMOs a bad rap. It is important to remember that not all of them are bad and that the term refers to anything altered by humans rather than by nature.

Non-GMO

Non-GMO food refers to all types of food that have been produced without the use of any type of food derived from GMO's. It's important to keep in mind that stores and brands will use both GMO and Non-GMO as a selling point, but it doesn't necessarily mean that either type of food is better, safer, or more nutritious for you. It's important to exercise discretion and do a little bit of research if you are concerned about a product that uses either of these terms.

Plant-Based

The term "plant-based" is rather self-explanatory. These foods are generally made to fit into specialized diets such as vegan or vegetarian. A "plant-based" food is made mostly of plant products; if you want to be sure that your food does not contain any meat or dairy, then look for the specific "vegetarian" or "vegan" label instead. Although the idea of plant-based foods sounds healthier, it's important to think critically and do your research, just like in your other food choices. Some companies will use fillers or increase harmful additives to replicate the flavors of common animal-based foods.

Vegan

Vegan foods are completely devoid of animal products (i.e., no meat, poultry, fish, eggs, or dairy). Much like plant-based foods, it is important to pay attention to labels. Just because something is advertised as vegan, does not mean it's healthy or good for you. With that said, vegan recipes are often nutrient packed, flavorful, and rather healthy. Most of them can be altered easily for other diets by adding meat or dairy to the dish.

Gluten-Free

Gluten is a type of protein that can be found in wheat and other types of grain. Gluten-free products are normally sought by those who suffer from celiac disease, or who are sensitive to gluten or allergic to wheat. This is another term that warrants caution if used as a sales tactic. Often companies will label products with these phrases, hoping people will automatically associate their foods with a healthy diet without further investigation.

An example of this might be placing a "Gluten Free Food" badge on a bag of dehydrated apple chips. Apples do not have gluten. They are naturally gluten free and just because these apple chips have a "healthy-looking" badge, doesn't mean that the company did not add an excessive amount of sugar or preservatives. Sales tactics such as these are rather common, which is why it's important to maintain a skeptical mind and always read food labels.

STORING FOOD

Storing your food properly is especially important when you are trying to make your groceries last longer. Below are list of common foods and where to store them.

Pantry and Cabinets

- Nuts
- Seeds
- All types of oils
- Grains
- Unsweetened and dried fruits
- All types of dry spices
- Canned and dried food
- Sweeteners
- Flour
- Sauces
- Dressings
- Snacks
- Coffee
- Chips

Freezer

- Meats you are not planning to eat immediately
- Vegetables

- Fruits
- Fish
- Ice cream
- Pre-made dinners

Refrigerator

It's a good idea to keep your refrigerator organized, so you know what you have available and can decrease waste. It's a good idea to:

- Store ingredients on the top shelf (milk, jars of olives, cheese, etc.)
- Store ready-to-eat meals on the second shelf (yogurt, snacks, and leftovers)
- Store veggies and fruit on the third shelf
- Store raw meat and fish on the bottom shelf. It's a good idea to line this shelf with absorbent towels in case liquid seeps from the packages.

REMEMBER: Cooked and fridge-stored poultry normally lasts around three to four days. Cooked and fridge-stored fish normally lasts around three to four days as well.

CHAPTER THREE:
DOCUMENTATION

DOCUMENTS YOU SHOULD HAVE

If you haven't already, there are a few documents you should acquire and keep safe. Although this section was written with American readers in mind, it's important to take inventory of common documentation needed in your specific country or state.

Birth Certificate

Birth certificates are one of the cornerstone documents used to prove citizenship. Although a parent or guardian might have taken care of this document for you in the past, it's important to obtain at least a copy of it for your personal records now that you are an adult. If for some reason this document is lost, it's a good idea to replace it as soon as possible so that you have it when you need it. Birth certificates are not managed federally, so you will need to know what state you were born in and request a replacement from the Vital Records offices of that specific state.

Social Security Card

This is another document that is usually safeguarded by a parent or guardian until adulthood. However, if for some reason you are not able to retrieve your Social Security card, you should apply for a replacement. Although it is rare for natural-born U.S. citizens, you may need to apply for an original Social Security card instead of a replacement. You can do this online at SSA.gov or by visiting your nearest Social Security Administration building. The documents required to apply for a Social Security card will vary depending on your situation.

Natural-Born Citizens will need to provide proof of their identity and age. This usually includes some form of photo identification, birth certificate, hospital record showing date of birth, or a U.S. passport. There are other options available if you are unable to locate any of these items. In those cases, it is highly recommended to talk to someone from your local Social Security Administration to find documents that meet the requirements to prove citizenship and age.

Immigrants will need to provide proof of their immigration status by bringing either their I-94 Arrival/Departure record, admission stamp in an unexpired foreign passport, I-766 Employment Authorization Document, EAD, work permit, Form I-551 (Lawful Permanent Resident Card, Machine Readable Immigrant Visa) and/or their unexpired foreign passport. As suggested above, it is always a good idea to call your local Social Security Administration to make sure you have all of the needed documents and learn what replacements are accepted by the offices.

Photo Identification

Although the most common form of photo ID is a driver's license, not everyone drives — especially those living in large cities with good public transportation infrastructures. Even if you don't drive, it's still wise to obtain a form of photo ID and keep it on your person at all times. Like driver's licenses, the DMV can issue a state ID. Until you are able to obtain an official state-issued photo ID, you should keep some form of identification that contains a photo of yourself, your first and last names, date of birth, expiration date, and signature. Sometimes a library card will work as a temporary fix, although there are many limitations to using this in lieu of an official photo ID.

Passports

Passports are required to travel outside of and re-enter your own country. Normally, to request a passport, you will need to fill out a form that can be found on governmental sites, and mail that form along with a color photo of your face (not a selfie) taken no more than six months prior. On the first page of your passport you will find your personal information, including your name, last name, date of birth, country of birth, nationality, and expiration date. The empty pages are reserved for stamps and visas whenever you travel abroad.

Generally speaking, passports follow stricter application requirements than other forms of identification. Although the application process will vary from country to country, the majority of passport applications will inquire about your citizenship, legal/criminal background, and basic information like your full name and birthdate. Some countries will require additional information regarding an applicant's family or have other restrictions. For example, in the U.S. there is a limitation regarding child support-related debt that can prevent an applicant from qualifying for a passport. The best policy is to check the government website for detailed information.

Usually, the process takes five to twelve weeks to complete, and first-time applicants are required to apply at approved facilities (like USPS), which are listed online. You'll need to have a passport photo already taken, which can be purchased at most stores that offer photo services (e.g., many drugstore chains). In addition to the photo, you'll need to have documents proving your identity and enough money in cash to cover the fees. These costs, documents, and turnaround times change periodically, so it is always a great idea to look up what you need online before driving to a qualified facility.

Passport Card

Passport cards require the same documentation as passports, but they are often cheaper and faster to receive than passports. Passport cards carry more power than a normal state photo ID but less power than a full passport book. The passport card will look similar to a driver's license, but it will allow you access to most of the Americas including Canada, Mexico, and some islands.

CHAPTER FOUR:
CONTRACTS

HOW TO READ CONTRACTS

Now that you've decided to live on your own, you will find yourself dealing with more and more contracts. Contracts are normally drawn up to put in writing agreements made jointly between two or more parties. There are many different types of contracts, such as those used for a lease, mortgage, or new job.

The first step is to understand the nature of the contract. Consider the importance of this contract. For example, sometimes contracts carry terms and agreements that can be disadvantageous to you. So if the contract is not vitally important, never feel obligated to sign it.

Read and pay attention to the terms and services of this contract, then what the other party expects of you. Terms are included in all types of contracts. Before signing any document, always take the time to read and understand the terms and conditions. If you disagree with any of the content, never hesitate to make your voice heard. A contract should only be signed if all parties are in agreement. If one party is not happy, the contract can always be rewritten.

Always ask for a copy of the document signed by both you and the other party to keep safely with you. Get into the good habit of rereading the contract with the other party. Never feel pressured and always remember that you are not obligated to sign any contract that you do not understand or are not

47

completely satisfied with. It is not easy to recognize a bad or bogus contract unless you are a trained lawyer. Some signs to look out for could be — being pushed or rushed into signing, the contract being nonnegotiable, or when you try to confront the other party you are reassured that things will be better once you sign. This last one is often a big red flag.

Another important to thing to remember is to never accept an oral agreement. Remember that everything needs to be put down in writing, so in case you ever need it in the future you have proofs and signatures on paper.

TIPS FOR READING CONTRACTS

Question What You're Reading

Every contract should be easy to read and understand. If there are portions that are convoluted or unnecessarily complicated, you should ask for clarification or reach out to a knowledgeable third party to help you translate the contracts. If there is a portion that seems more complex than the rest of the contract, this could be a red flag indicating that there is something being intentionally hidden by the overly complex descriptions.

Identify All the Parties Involved

If the contract at hand references holding companies or subsidiaries, it's a good idea to pay attention and investigate these further. A subsidiary is any company that is controlled by a holding company and a holding company is created to hold (and control) more than one company. In other words, if the holding company is listed on the contract, then it includes multiple smaller companies. It is important to know who you are signing a contract with and often this can be concealed by listing parent companies.

Important Terms to Know

An **indemnity clause** protects a party from being sued. A common positive example of this might occur if you take out a large loan from a bank. Sometimes the bank will offer an indemnity clause for an additional fee to protect your loved ones from having to take over your loan if you were to die before it is paid off. In a negative example, an indemnity clause could protect someone from being sued for doing something like selling your information to another company or person, which is why it is so important to pay attention whenever this term shows up.

Mandatory arbitration means that if you were to try to sue a company or raise any complaints against the contract holder, you wouldn't be able to take it to court. An arbitrator can either be a single person or a group of people who will make a decision about the dispute. This is not necessarily a bad thing, but it is something that deserves attention. Many companies will want to handle disputes through arbitration because it is more private and discreet than a full court case.

Another term to pay close attention to is **breach of contract**, which refers to what happens if the terms of the contract are not upheld. This is important to know and understand in case something goes wrong. You should be well versed in the repercussions of not holding up your end of the deal, and likewise, you should know what will happen and how you can take action if the other person does the same.

TERMS OF SERVICE

In this day and age, you've probably already signed many Terms of Service documents. They are required for everything from social media accounts to phone games. Even though these texts come up frequently and are often long-winded, it's important to read through them before signing up for something. The most common thing hidden in these contracts is the right to keep and sell your personal information. Often, companies will sell your personal information to a third party that will then either sell it to individuals or large companies that use the data for marketing. This might include information such as your name, birthday, physical address, phone number, and gender. Or, the terms of service might allow for an even larger invasion of privacy that extends to accessing your photos.

If you have ever tried to do an internet search on someone, you have probably seen the repercussions of these Terms of Service contracts in action. Some websites offer information on individuals for a small fee. If you sign up for products or services that collect and sell your data, it means that anyone could potentially have access to your personal details for as little as a dollar. This is a serious potential threat to your privacy.

Another huge issue is allowing companies legal access to your photos. If they can sell your name and address, they most likely have no moral qualms doing the same with your private photo collection.

So, when reading terms of service, pay attention to:

- Whether or not a third party or affiliate will have access to your information
- Whether or not you can sign up without sharing your information
- Whether or not you can sue them or take legal action if something goes wrong
- Is the Term of Service requesting a waiving of rights or release of information?

Despite how cumbersome reading Terms of Service can be, it is extremely important to take the time to read them closely and protect yourself from predators both online and in real life. If you practice doing this every single time, you will get faster and more efficient at deciphering what you are signing. There are also many articles available online on how to read Terms of Service faster and more efficiently.

CHAPTER FIVE:
CLOTHING

It's important to learn how to take care of your clothes and shoes properly to extend their lifespan and keep them in nice condition. Before diving into learning how to take care of your clothes, it's a good idea to understand fabric types and how they are made as you'll want to treat each kind of fabric differently. There are two main types of fabric: natural and synthetic. Synthetic fabric comes from materials that are man-made, while natural fabrics are made from materials that occur naturally (e.g., cotton). Fabrics are processed differently to create different garments, and it's important to know whether they are woven or knitted as that will affect how you might mend and wash them. Woven fabrics have yarn laced both horizontally and vertically while knitted fabrics have threads interconnected to each other in a series of special stitches.

COMMON FABRIC TYPES

Chiffon

Chiffon is usually made of silk, nylon, or polyester. This fabric is usually used to make scarves, blouses, and formal dresses. The best way to wash this fabric is either by hand or in the washing machine under a gentle cycle, with cold water. Do not iron or leave in the sun.

Cotton

This is the most common material used in making clothing. Cotton can be washed and dried by hand or a machine.

Denim

Denim is usually used to make jeans and is mainly made of cotton fabric. Although it is a tough fabric, the best way to wash denim is using a delicate cycle with cold water to avoid shrinking. The best way to dry denim is to let it air-dry, but if you want to use the dryer make sure to select a low heat and gentle cycle. Traditionally, denim jeans were frozen to kill germs rather than washed. Some people still practice this, but it is only recommended for true denim jeans rather than a blended fabric.

Lace

Lace is usually made with cotton and synthetic fibers. The type of thread requires a gentle wash with cold water. The best way to dry lace material is to wrap it in a clean dry towel.

Leather

Leather is derived from animal skin such as cow, lamb, or even crocodile. Leather clothing is long lasting but must be cared for properly; review the instructions that came with your garment. Leather should never be dried in the dryer. Hang the piece of clothing to let it air-dry.

Linen

Linen is made of natural material and is stronger than cotton. Wash linen in lukewarm water on a gentle cycle. Linen can be air-dried or placed in the dryer.

Satin

Satin was originally made of silk, though now it's made with polyester and rayon. Satin must be washed by hand or on a cold and delicate cycle. If you hand-wash your satin, do not wring or twist the cloth as this will make it lose its shape. The best way to dry satin is air-drying, though you can also use your dryer. If you choose the latter, make sure it's on low heat.

Silk

Silk is made from the silkworm's cocoon and originated in China, South Asia, and Europe. The best way to wash silk is to let the garment soak in cold water with some drops of detergent. Let your silk air-dry and avoid the sunlight as sun can damage the color of the garment.

Synthetics

Synthetics are produced by man-made fibers. The best way to wash synthetics is with lukewarm water, since synthetic fabric is sensitive to heat and can be ruined by excessively hot water. To dry synthetics either air-dry or use the dryer at the lowest temperature.

Velvet

Velvet is made of silk, cotton, or synthetic fibers. When washing velvet, always use cold water and avoid using the dryer. Opt for air-drying instead.

Wool

Wool is fabric that is derived from the fleece of sheep, goats, rabbits, and other animals. To wash wool, select the gentle cycle and use cold water. Using hot water will cause your wool clothing to shrink. The best option to dry wool is to air-dry, avoiding direct sunlight and high heat.

WHAT TO DO WITHOUT A DRYER

Not everyone has a clothes dryer, and that's perfectly fine. People have been finding other ways to effectively dry out fabrics for millennia prior to the invention of the dryer! Here are some tricks and tips to help you dry your clothes when you don't have a drying machine available.

Leave your clothes in the washer for an extra spin cycle. This will ensure all the excess water is removed from your clothes before you try to dry them.

Hang your wet clothes on a drying rack. With sturdier fabrics, you can place your drying rack outside in the sunlight, which will allow your clothing to dry more quickly. If the weather isn't agreeable, or your clothing is very delicate, you can keep the drying rack inside. Your clothes will dry wherever you place them, though it may take a bit longer inside.

For more gentle fabrics like lace and fine wool, you can dry the garment by placing it flat on a dry towel and then rolling the towel up and setting it somewhere safe until the garment is completely dry.

Place your damp clothing in a dry towel and then iron it. The heat from the iron will allow the water to evaporate while the dry towel will serve as a protectant to your garment, stopping the hot water from ruining your cloth.

You can also install a stainless-steel retractable line inside or outside. If you do this inside, choose a well-ventilated room so that the air flow will help dry your clothes.

TIPS FOR STAIN REMOVAL

Not everyone sees it this way, but buying clothes is a kind of investment, especially if you purchase expensive clothing. We want the things we buy to last as long as possible. Sometimes daily living and carelessness can cause us to stain our clothes. Some types of stains are easy to remove, while others are notoriously difficult. Here are some useful home remedies that can be effective when it comes to getting rid of stubborn stains from your clothes, and the best thing is that these tips don't require using any chemicals. Below is a list of substances that may stain your clothes, and suggestions for how to remove those particular stains.

Oil

Place some dish detergent over the stain along with some sea salt. Gently scrub the sea salt over the stain, then rinse with warm water.

Blood

The basic rule for bloodstains is the earlier the better. A fresh stain is almost always easier to remove, and very cold water tends to work well for fabrics stained with blood. Be sure you blot the stain with cold water and a wet cloth or paper towel — blot, don't rub! Rubbing will make the stain larger.

If the blood is already dry, then your best remedy will be hydrogen peroxide. Pour just a few drops on the stained area and let it work. If bubbles emerge, this means the remedy is working. At this point, wipe with an absorbent cloth and rinse with cold water, never hot!

Pen Ink

Again, the sooner you treat these stains, the better. You can dab the stain with vinegar and let it sit for a few hours, then wash in a regular washing machine cycle.

Sweat

Vinegar is one of the best choices for treating sweat stains. Dilute it with water then dab it onto the affected area. After that, soak the garment in cold water for a few hours and then wash as normal.

Fruit

For fruit stains, rub the fabric with vinegar diluted in water or a mixture of salt, lemon, and vinegar. If the stain is more stubborn, an alternative remedy is hydrogen peroxide.

Grass

While the stain is still fresh, dab the affected area with pure alcohol. On more delicate garments, use hydrogen peroxide diluted with two drops of water. You can also dab the area with a little vinegar and let it sit for an hour before washing the garment in a machine.

Rust

You can remove rust stains by applying fine salt and lemon juice to the affected area and then rinsing it with cold water. Another alternative is rubbing baking soda on the fabric with the help of a damp brush.

Nail Polish

Gently blot the stain with nail polish remover. Use lots of cotton and change the cotton often. Be careful with the type of fabric, as acetone can fade the fabric's color.

Coffee

Surprisingly, shaving foam can work wonders on coffee stains. Scrub the garment with a brush and proceed with normal washing. Another alternative is using sparkling water mixed with lemon juice or water diluted with vinegar.

Wax

To remove wax, soak the garment in warm water to soften the wax. Or, use an old toothbrush and gently scrub the fabric with alcohol. You can also run a hot iron over it, being careful to place parchment paper between the iron and the fabric. This helps to melt the wax so that it's easier to remove.

Chocolate

Mix a teaspoon of soap with a dab of lukewarm water, apply to the chocolate stain, and let it sit for thirty minutes before rinsing.

Eggs

You can either let the garment soak in cold water for an hour or treat the stain with hydrogen peroxide before machine washing it.

Wine

Depending on the type of fabric, pour boiling water on the stain or rub it with sparkling water. If the wine stain is set and dry, apply toothpaste to the stain before washing.

Tomato

To remove tomato stains, dab the stain with vinegar or a mixture made of equal parts water and soda.

TYPES OF SHOES

Shoes are made using different types of materials, including:

Leather: animal skin that has retained the original fiber structure, and treated so that it does not rot.

Coated leather: leather that has been coated or laminated with another material. The coating is made to be less than one-third the thickness of the product. A thin layer of leather can be laminated with material such as cardboard, rubber, or cloth, among other options.

Textile material: can be natural, synthetic, or nonwoven.

Other material: such as rubber, cork, polymer and wood.

HOW TO WASH SHOES

Each type of shoe requires its own method of washing properly so as to avoid damage.

Sneakers

The best method for washing sneakers is with warm water and soap. Scrub the dirtiest parts with an old toothbrush so that you can reach even the most hidden or hard-to-reach places. To clean the most difficult spots you can use the so-called "magic sponge" that is normally used to clean walls of dirt.

Canvas or Fabric

The best method for cleaning shoes made of canvas or fabric is to use cold water with a delicate detergent, adding a few drops of fabric softener from time to time. For optimal washing, it's best to let the shoes soak for six hours and then brush energetically. Once washed, let the shoes dry naturally, making sure that they are well opened and away from heat sources and direct sunlight. Wash the shoes by hand and not in a washing machine to prevent the aggressive nature of the washing machine from deteriorating the rubber bottom.

Leather

To avoid halos on the leather after getting leather shoes wet, wet the entire shoe with a damp cloth and then fill the inside of the shoe with kitchen paper or newspaper to help it keep its shape. Leave the shoes to dry on their side away from the sun and heat sources, ideally in a well-ventilated area so that moisture will evaporate more easily. To do a routine cleaning, however, start by dusting the shoes. Then wipe the leather with an appropriate cream for leather shoes, applying a little at a time so that the material can absorb the product.

Suede

Suede shoes are particularly delicate and often require specific products. If you are without these products and absolutely need to clean your shoes, you can use warm water with a dash of shampoo and a generous dose of softener. This method is very useful for stains caused by rain. For a routine cleaning, simply remove the dust with a bristle or an iron spatula.

Painted

Painted shoes are as easy to clean as they are prone to getting dirty more easily than other materials. These kinds of shoes need to look clean and shiny at all times to show their beauty. Just use a cloth lightly soaked in milk. The goal is not to scratch the shoes, so never use the brushes you would use for leather shoes. As a final step, always remember to dry the shoes thoroughly with a clean cloth and never let the leather be excessively wet.

Shoes are delicate and can be easily ruined by daily wearing. Sometimes using natural ingredients can play a role in keeping our shoes looking young. So, here are some other small tricks and natural remedies to clean your shoes without the use of harsh materials or chemical substances.

Vinegar can be an important ally, especially when it comes to cleaning tennis shoes. This ingredient is perfect for whitening the edge of the sneaker. The best vinegar to use is pure and concentrated vinegar diluted with water.

Baking soda mixed with water can produce a smooth cream that can be applied to shoes with light tints. This natural remedy can be used on canvas shoes.

Cornstarch is very useful for removing grease stains from shoes. The first step is to sprinkle the stain with cornstarch, which is easy to trace. Then cover the affected area with paper towels and place a weight on top of the shoe. Let it sit for about twenty minutes and proceed to wash off the starch using a soapy sponge. Finally, rinse with a dampened cloth.

Orange peels and tea bags are excellent natural remedies to remove odor from shoes, leaving behind a nice scent. After washing your shoes with a damp cloth, let them dry, and then place small pieces of orange peel or a tea bag inside the shoe overnight.

To polish faux leather shoes, an excellent ally is **olive oil** combined with a few drops of **lemon**. Rub the shoes with a cotton cloth or sponge using the mixture. Leave for a few minutes and then wipe off with a clean cloth.

Another amazing remedy is salt and soap to use for yellowed work shoes. With the help of a brush, remove the dirt. Before rinsing, rub coarse salt all over the outer and inner surfaces of the sneakers. Leave for one hour, and then rinse with cold water and detergent.

Salt and milk are a useful combination; the milk makes the salt even more effective. In a basin, combine the salt and the milk. Soak your shoes in the liquid for three hours. After that, rub the shoes with the soap and let them dry.

For soil and dirt stains, you can make a spray with 2/3 cup water, 1/3 cup apple cider vinegar, and 2 teaspoons baking soda. Spray the mixture on the stained surface and leave for about five minutes. Don't worry about the amount of liquid you spray — the more the better. Afterward, with a damp cloth, remove the liquid from the shoe.

In case of stubborn dirt and bad smell, you can clean your sneakers with baking soda and soap. Common dish detergent and a tablespoon of common baking soda is fine. Scrub the outside of the shoe with a toothbrush, rinse and let dry.

Laces: wash the laces by hand and with warm water, remove them from the water and then soak them in a mixture created from soap and baking soda. This method will also remove odors.

MENDING YOUR CLOTHES

If you have a ripped piece of clothing, know that you don't need a sewing machine to fix it. All you need is the right needle and enough thread. In order to do this effectively, you must at least know the difference between the main types of needles.

Sharps are an all-purpose type of needles. They are medium length and have what is called a round eye, where you will be putting your thread.

Leather needles are a specific type of needle used to cut through leather, which is typically tougher and thicker than cotton fabric.

Ballpoint needles are suitable when working on softer fabric such as a T-shirt. They are gentle enough to not damage the fibers.

Darning needles are perfect to fix holes in sweaters, jackets, or wool materials.

When you are trying to mend a hole, the first step is to always turn your garment inside out, that way you'll have a better chance to hide the stitching.

1. Choose the correct needle and color of thread.

2. Thread the needle.
3. Make sure you have enough thread and tie a knot at the end, to ensure it will stay put.
4. Start by pushing the needle through the fabric as close as possible to the hole, so that you're not taking up too much fabric and it will look more natural. Pull the needle until the knot reaches the fabric.
5. Cross your needle through the hole and pull again until it's tight enough.
6. Repeat these last two steps until the hole starts to close. Remember when pulling do so in a way that doesn't cause the fabric to overlap.
7. Once the whole is completely patched, create a loop with your thread and stick the needle through the loop. Repeat the process once you are confident the stitching is secured.

If the hole in your clothing is too big, remember that you can always fix it by patching with another material to cover the hole.

CHAPTER SIX:
HOME APPLIANCES

THE REFRIGERATOR

Your fridge is easily one of the most important appliances in your house because it stores your food. Therefore, ensuring proper maintenance of your refrigerator is very important.

Setting the Right Temperature

First of all, you want to make sure you set both your fridge and your freezer at the right temperature. For your fridge, the recommended temperature is 4°C or 39.2°F, while for your freezer, it must be below 0°C or 32°F. If you are storing meat it would be even better if you set the temperature to -18°C or 0°F.

Proper Storage

Make sure you always cover any food you decide to store in your fridge and you arrange it all properly to not block any vents.

Defrost the Freezer

Always empty the accumulated frost in your freezer, as accumulated frost can cause a waste of energy, hence a higher electrical bill at the end of each month.

Placement

Make sure your fridge is not placed completely up against the wall. By leaving some space between the appliance and the wall, your refrigerator will run more efficiently.

The Condenser

Make sure to take time to clean your refrigerator's condenser. This is because there can be a buildup of dust or dirt that will not allow your refrigerator to dispense heat properly and the cooling process will not be efficient.

Water Dispenser

If your fridge also has a water dispenser, make sure to change your water filter every six months. Not replacing your water filter might cause you to intake dangerous pollutants that can travel through the pipes and tubes.

THE MICROWAVE

When you were a child, you probably were told many times that certain things do not belong in the microwave. Let's review a list of what must never be put in the microwave, along with how to defrost your food without burning it.

NEVER USE IN A MICROWAVE:

Aluminum foil can spark, burn quickly, and can be a fire hazard.

Paper bags can release toxins and can be harmful to your health if heated.

Plastic containers that are not microwave safe can melt, start fires, or release microplastics into your food.

Hard-boiled eggs can explode due to the microwave's high temperature.

Styrofoam, once heated, can melt through your food causing the release of chemicals. It can also start a fire from melting and getting too hot.

Anything metal, as it will spark and can easily start a fire.

Defrosting Frozen Food

First and foremost, remove any packaging before you place your food in the microwave. There are different heating recommendations for each type and quantity of food. Note that every microwave is different, so the information below is meant to be a starting point. You'll have to test with your own microwave and adjust the cooking times accordingly.

For chicken and poultry: set your microwave to defrost, at about two minutes per pound of poultry. For example, three pounds of poultry will require a total of six minutes in the microwave.

For beef: set your microwave to the defrost setting or to 50% power. Set the timer to two or three minutes, making sure you flip the meat every 45 seconds.

Fish: set your microwave to the defrost setting or to 30% power. Set the timer to two minutes, making sure you flip your fish every 30 seconds.

Remember, if you decide to defrost your meat in the microwave, you will have to cook it immediately afterward, as it often happens that some pieces might be accidentally cooked while being thawed inside the appliance.

THE STOVE

We all know that stoves use heat to cook our meals. There are two main types of stoves. The traditional stove, at least for the vast majority of countries around the world, is the gas stove. A gas stove uses a supply of gas to create an adjustable flame at each burner. The heat that is generated by the flame is transmitted to the food being cooked.

The other common type of stove is the electric stove, a cooktop that works through electric current (not gas). An electric stove contains internal coils that are powered by electricity and by induction transfers energy, or heat, directly to the bottom of the pan, without the presence of a combustion process.

So what's the difference between the two? The basic difference is precisely how heat is transmitted. The electric cooktop may be more convenient because it has more functions, but a gas stove is faster at heating food because of the way the heat is distributed.

How to Use an Oven

If you've taken a look at the knobs and buttons that control your oven, you've probably noticed there are many options for how to use the oven to heat or cook your food. Developing a familiarity with each of these functions will help you to make the best choices when you are trying to bake your cake or cook your roast beef.

Conventional cooking uses both the upper and lower heating elements of the oven. This type of oven cooking is suitable for breads, fatty meats, or casseroles.

Fan-forced cooking disperses heat through the internal fan. In this way, heat is distributed equally inside the oven. This type of cooking is perfect for beef, lamb, and very large meals.

Bake is the self-explanatory setting you want to use when you are making breads, cakes, or other baked goods.

Broil only activates the top part of the heating mechanism, so all of the heat comes from the top of the oven down onto the top of the food. This mode is mostly used to sear food or melt toppings.

Warm is used for food that is already cooked and that you want to keep warm until the time it is served.

Many ovens also have a "clean" function, which, when selected, will lock the oven to prevent it from being opened while it heats to a very high temperature. Afterward, it will be easier to do the final cleaning that you will have to do yourself with the use of a clean rag and water or the correct cleaner.

THE TELEVISION

It is likely that, at this point, you rely mostly on the internet and streaming services to watch television shows and movies. However, your TV may have lots of cables available (typically found on the back or side of the unit), and you may wonder what they're for. Let's review them together.

Depending on the television you have, it's very likely that you have some of the following ports.

HDMI: one of the most popular cables, which when connected to your television and another external software, such as a computer, allows you to see the other software's screen reflected directly on your television.

S-Video: used mostly in the 1990s, it is used to transmit video to your television—only video, no sound.

The component connection: normally made up of three wires of three different colors. Each color matches the color of the input to the TV, and each wire has its own task. These were used, and are still used today to connect DVD players to the television.

The USB port, which receives connections with a USB cable.

Last, but not least, you will connect your power cable in order for your TV to function.

THE WASHING MACHINE

The washing machine is the appliance you'll use to wash your clothes along with the specific stain-removal tips provided earlier. In addition to making life significantly easier, being familiar with your washing machine is also important for the life of your clothes and of the machine itself. Listed below are a few common elements in the process of washing clothes.

Pre-washing is done with the appropriate detergent placed in the appropriate compartment before the washing machine itself is turned on.

Washing is done based on the temperature and duration set through the appropriate program.

Rinsing of the clothes occurs after they have been washed, to remove the soap from the fabric.

Centrifuge or the **spin cycle** rotates the clothes at a high speed within the machine in order to remove excess water before draining.

Regardless of the type of washing machine you have, whether it's among the most modern or an older one, these are the functions you will most commonly find:

Delicates: suitable for washing delicate fabrics such as lace or silk. Delicate programs usually use soaking before washing and temperatures are lower.

Quick wash: often used for quick washing of garments such as bedding. This type of washing uses more water and higher temperatures.

Wool: useful for specific fabrics — including, of course, wool — this program uses a water temperature that does not exceed 30°C so as not to ruin the fabric

Some tips for keeping your washing machine running:

Keep it clean, and remember to also clean the special compartments where the detergents are added.

Rinse off soap residue using the detergents provided for washing machine cleaning.

A good practice to follow is to wash your empty washing machine with hot water, vinegar, and baking soda, which will eliminate possible odors and the presence of mold.

THE DRYER

If you own a clothes dryer and intend to use it often, it's a good idea to know its main functions, as not all clothes can be put in the dryer. Given the high temperatures the dryer uses, it can be damaging to some fabrics, especially those that are more delicate. Depending on the type of dryer you own, you may have many functions to select from, especially if you have one of the newest models. These are some of the most common functions you will find in this appliance:

Delicate or gentle cycle: generates medium heat that is perfect for more delicate clothes, such as silk.

Permanent press: this program may turn out to be the best choice for most of the clothes you use on a daily basis. This type of program is perfect for those who do not like ironing.

Regular or automatic: this type of program uses a very high temperature, and you can usually manually set the time duration you prefer.

Steam cycle (found mostly in new generation dryers): remember that this program will not dry your clothes because it does not use high temperatures but simply steams your clothing to remove creases.

Also, it's a good idea to follow these tips to make sure that your dryer will last several years:

Clean the lint screen and cavity before every load. A neglected lint screen is one of the most common causes of dryer fires. It's a good idea to clean this out before every load. There is also another unofficial lint trap on the dryer vent leading to the outside of your house. It's a good idea to clean this regularly as well because lint is extremely flammable.

Clean the drum once a month, even if the inside of your dryer looks clean. This includes the lip around the door's seal and any vents.

Do not overload your dryer. This is a good way to overwhelm your dryer and wear out the parts faster. If you do not want to pay for repairs or fry your dryer, it's a good idea not to stuff it as full as possible. Another problem that comes with overloading your dryer is the amount of time it will take to get your clothes dry. You are more likely to need to run your clothes for multiple cycles if you add too many into the drum. This will increase your electricity costs in the long run and if you are using coin-op laundry, this can become more expensive than just drying smaller loads.

CHAPTER SEVEN:
COMMON HOUSE ISSUES AND EASY FIXES

CLOGGED DRAINS

If your drains are clogged, you can easily follow one of these steps before running to the store and buying any product.

First, remove all the standing water immediately to avoid mold and bacteria.

Second, remove any visible and obvious object that might be the cause of the blockage.

Once you have followed these two steps, if your drain still seems to be clogged, here are some tips and tricks you can use:

- Use a plunger to remove other objects that you might not be able to see.
- Pour boiling water with soap into the drain.
- Pour vinegar and baking soda into the drain.
- Use a plumbing snake to clear out any possible blockage from your drain.
- Use a specific product for drain clogs, which you can purchase at most grocery stores.

DRIPPING FAUCETS

Many different things can cause a faucet to leak. Before getting to work, it's helpful to know what the problems with your faucet might be.

Defective O-ring—The O-ring is a small disc attached to the stem screw that holds the faucet handle in place. If the leak is coming from the sink handle, the O-ring is the likely cause of the leak. Fixing your problem will simply require changing the O-ring.

Valve seat—If the leak comes from the spout, the problem may be in the valve seat that connects the faucet to the spout. This problem may be caused by water sediment accumulation. To avoid this kind of problem, clean the valve seat regularly.

Worn washers—If the leakage comes from the spout, another cause may be a worn washer. To solve your problem, simply replace the worn washer.

Worn gaskets—Just like valves, gaskets can be corroded by the accumulation of water sediment. As in the previous case, replacing the worn gasket will quickly solve your problem.

Water pressure—If the faucet tends to drip only at certain times or when you move the handles in a certain way, the cause may be the water pressure in your home.

Loose parts—The adjusting ring and pre-seal nuts in the flow screw may become loose over time, causing the sink handle to come off. Tightening the pre-seal nut or replacing it will solve your leakage problem.

Broken parts—If the leak is coming from the pipes under your sink, the cause might be a broken pipe or fitting. In this case, the best solution is to rely on a professional.

Once you have identified the source of your problem, the first step to fixing it is to turn off the water. Normally, the valve to do this is located under the faucet. Once you've turned off the water, open your faucet so that the remaining water can completely drain out.

LEAKY PIPES

If you have a leaky pipe, you can select from several possible solutions:

You can use water pipe epoxy, one of the most common temporary solutions. Remember, this solution is not permanent, but it will help you keep the situation under control until a plumber arrives, or if the problem is relatively minor.

Pipe wraps, like epoxy, will harden after being applied to the damaged part, thus covering any holes or cracks present in the pipe.

You can use pipe clamps, which must be the same size as the leaking pipe. All you will need to do is line up the rubber gasket over the leak, put the clamp around the gasket, and make sure it is tight by tightening the bolts.

Before you select and proceed with any of these steps, however, be sure to close the pipe so that the material can adhere properly to the pipe. If there is water present, dry the part you will need to repair.

RUNNING TOILETS

Running toilets are a very common problem that you'll almost certainly encounter at some point. Some of the most likely causes include:

Refill tube malfunction—This component serves to fill up your tank, and its top is supposed to always stay above the water's level. If this doesn't happen, you might hear your toilet running intermittently. To fix it, you will have to shut off the water and flush the toilet one last time to completely empty out the water tank. Second, remove the lid and the float ball. Use a towel to remove any remaining water inside of the tank. Once you are done drying the tank, use a wrench to unscrew the mounting net that holds the old assembly in place and take out the old valve. Adjust your new mounting to ensure that the ball will be above the toilet's overflow tube. To install the new valve, simply insert it where you have already taken out the old assembly and tighten the lock net below. Attach the refill tube to the overflow pipe. Finally, reconnect the supply line to your toilet.

Float ball malfunction—This ball's function is to close the valve once the tank is filled. If the ball is not properly aligned, this might not allow the valve to close completely and water will keep running.

Your gasket is worn—The seal between the tank and the bowl can become worn out. The old seal is normally placed at the bottom of the assembly of the overflow. Remove the worn valve by simply pulling it. Don't worry if it breaks, as the important thing is that you take it out. Replace the old seal with the new one.

LOW WATER PRESSURE

If your pressure water is low, the first thing you'll want to do is check your valves. If your valve is only partially opened, this could be the cause of your low water pressure. To increase the pressure, simply open your valve by turning the handle. If you have a water pressure reducing valve, it can be readjusted to increase the water's pressure.

CIRCUIT BREAKER
TRIPPING

If the circuit breaker trips, one of the most common reasons is excessive use of electricity. To avoid this type of problem, be sure to turn off any appliances you're not using.

REPLACING LIGHTBULBS

If you want to replace a burned-out bulb, start by identifying the bulb type—its particular shape and size. Not all bulbs are the same and each has its own function. Next, determine the amount of light you need for this particular light fixture. For example, an overhead light in a room that tends to be dim will need to be bright, while the small lamp next to your bed might not need such a powerful bulb. Third, select the coloration you want:

2700-2800K: gives off a light-yellow color.

3000-3200K: the light is slightly yellow but is brighter.

3500-4000K: the light is neutral and bright white.

There are also **LED bulbs** on the market that can change color, not only from yellow to white, but also to other shades.

As a final step, select the right type of bulb:

Energy-saving (halogen): have a lower watt use.

Compact fluorescents: often has a curly shape.

LEDs: considered the most efficient option compared to incandescent bulbs and can last more than twice as long.

Smart bulbs: these are often LED bulbs that can be connected to control systems (such as your cell phone). Their function is different from the typical bulb; in addition to illuminating a space, they can change to different colors.

DYSFUNCTIONAL LIGHT SWITCHES

There are many possible reasons for your dysfunctional light switches and you may be able to fix some of them without having to call an expert, though always remember that serious precautions are needed when making electrical repairs.

There could be a broken mechanism in your light switch, which is easily solved by replacing your old light switch with a new one.

If you have a loose light switch, remove the switch screws, and then remove the switch. Tighten up the screws that you find underneath the switch and then simply remount the switch on the wall.

Sometimes the reason for a dysfunctional light switch is a light bulb that has simply run its course. In this case, all you will have to do is change the light bulb.

FIRE ALARMS

Let's start with the fact that having fire alarms (smoke detectors) in your house is very important and will be life-saving in case of fire. You've probably witnessed a fire alarm going off seemingly for no reason, but that's not really the case. Some fire alarms will go off if they detect carbon monoxide in the house. Carbon monoxide is an odorless gas that can lead to poisoning. Other times, your fire alarms go off simply because of a malfunction, such as batteries that need to be replaced. Other reasons might be that dirt or dust are covering the sensor chamber, there's been a power interruption, or the presence of insects in the sensor chamber.

WALLS

How to Use a Stud Finder

Let's start by clarifying what a stud is. A stud is a beam that supports the frame of a house. Studs are normally placed behind drywall. If you are planning to hang something on the wall, especially if the object is heavy, the best way to do so while avoiding unnecessary holes in your wall is to find the position of the studs in your wall. To do so, you can buy a stud finder at any store or online.

How to Make a Hole in the Wall Correctly

If you want to place a hole in your wall, start by choosing the correct bit. You don't want to make a hole that will be too big or too small for your screws. When drilling holes in your walls there are some spots you should always avoid drilling into:

- Avoid drilling above or below a light switch or an outlet.
- If you are going to drill into a wall in your bathroom, make sure you are not drilling through a plumbing pipe.

If you are drilling through drywall, make sure you first identify the position of the studs. Drywall is typically a thinner material that can't carry heavy loads. This is why it's best to drill through a stud, which is thicker and much stronger.

Mark the area where you are going to drill and use a level to make sure the markings are even.

Start drilling into your wall, adding pressure gradually, making sure you keep your hand firm and straight. Once you're done, slowly pull the bit out of the whole.

How to Fix a Hole in Drywall

Almost all holes can be patched, especially if you are working with drywall.

A small hole can be patched with putty or spackle. Using a putty knife, fill in the hole.

For bigger holes you can use a mesh adhesive patch, which can be bought at the store, and that is easily applied to the hole. First, clean up the edges of the hole. Apply the patch, smoothing it out to make sure that there are no creases or wrinkles. Apply the spackling paste onto the patch with the putty knife, making sure you apply it through the holes of the patch first, and then throughout the entire surface of the patch.

THE TOOLBOX

Having a complete toolbox is important, especially if you are living by yourself. You never know what can break at any given time and what you'll have to fix when you least expect it, so having and knowing how to use a toolbox is important when it comes to home repairs and self-sufficiency. Let's go over what should be kept inside your toolbox.

Ratcheting screwdriver: This type of tool is useful when you have to make multiple turns, for example of a screw. This type of tool will allow you to reposition your hand each time without having to remove the screwdriver from its position.

Drill and drill bits: A drill is used to drill holes into surfaces such as walls. Every drill has to be attached to a drill bit in order to carry out its function. A drill bit is the tip end that is attached to the drill. Drill bits come in different sizes and lengths according to the application. Some bits are suitable only for drilling into wood, while others are best if used on tile or glass.

Stud finder: This tool is important especially if the walls in your house is made of drywall. It will allow you to find the studs behind the walls, into which you can safely drill holes — for example, to hang a painting or a heavy mirror.

Hammer: A hammer is a tool that has a heavy metal head and can be used for tasks that require force, for example to break though materials or to drive nails into a wall.

Pry bar: More commonly known as crowbar, a pry bar can be used to pull to objects apart.

Hex key set: Also known as Allen key, this is used to drive bolts in or out, or to turn screws with hexagonal shapes.

Adjustable wrench: This is an open-ended wrench that can be adjusted in size.

Pliers: Pliers come in a variety of shapes and are multipurpose. They are commonly used to twist or cut wires.

Tape measure: This is probably one of the most important tools that should be in your toolbox, simply because when it comes to home decorations or renovations, using a tape measure is essential. It allows you to accurately measure your space and whatever materials you're working with, and you'll need it for everything from hanging a picture to choosing a rug.

Putty knife: A putty knife is used to apply soft materials into cracks or holes. For example, if you are using a spackle compound to patch a hole in your wall, you can use a putty knife to do so.

Screwdrivers come in different shapes. The most common are:

- Philipps screwdriver, or crosshead screwdriver
- Star screwdriver
- Hex screwdriver
- Insulated screwdriver or safety screwdriver
- Flathead screwdriver
- Square screwdriver

Nails are used for multiple purposes according to their size and shape.

- Common nails: As the name suggests, this is the most common type of nail you'll come across and it is often used for projects that require a sturdy support.
- Finishing nails: These are normally thin and smooth and, as the name suggests, are used to do finishing work, for example for wood projects.

91

- Drywall nails: These nails are sturdier, they are used for drywall.

CHAPTER EIGHT:
HOUSE CLEANING

LEARN WHAT PRODUCTS TO USE

When it comes down to cleaning your house, water and soap are not always enough. It's a good idea to keep these other items on hand:

- Rubber gloves
- All-purpose cleaner
- Glass cleaner
- Baking soda
- Salt
- Vinegar
- Sponges and/or microfiber cloths
- A broom
- A mop
- A vacuum (especially if you have carpet or rugs)

DON'T FORGET HIDDEN SPACES

When you are cleaning your house, it's easy to forget about the small and hidden spaces, because your focus tends to be on the bigger picture. Here is a list of all those surfaces that might usually be forgotten:

- Trash can

- Kitchen range
- Hood filter
- Dishwasher
- Underneath the fridge
- The back of the toilet
- Bath fan grill
- Computer keyboards
- Toothbrush holders
- Shower caddy
- Toilet brush and holder
- Faucet aerator
- Inside drains

CLEANING TIPS AND TRICKS

Clean your mirrors and windows using vinegar and newspaper.

Clean your showerhead by soaking it in vinegar.

Place a glass of water and some slices of lemon in your **microwave** and let it run for a couple of minutes. This will make it easier for you to remove the tougher leftovers from the interior microwave surface.

Toothpaste is not only good for your teeth, it can be a good product to use on **floor stains.**

Baking soda also works as a **limescale remover** and it is effective in **removing traces of mold**. To use baking soda as a limescale remover, simply make a paste with three parts baking soda and one part water, spread on a sponge, and rub gently over the encrusted surface.

In the case of particularly **dirty pots and pans**, fill them with a solution of warm water, coarse salt, and lemon juice. You can leave the mixture to work for half an hour and then proceed with normal washing.

To protect clothes from moths, just prepare a small cotton bag with lavender, cloves, cinnamon sticks, and bay leaves, then close it up and place it in closets or drawers.

Combining water, baking soda, and white vinegar makes a powerful **degreaser** useful for **cleaning bathroom fixtures or the kitchen**.

A dry cotton cloth allows you to quickly **remove dust** from knickknacks and wooden furniture (without using specific products).

When you bake something in the oven, pans tend to crust. **To get rid of the baked-on residue**, soak the baking sheet in hot water and cover it with a tea towel. Wait half an hour and you will see that it will quickly degrease.

If you have white sofas, chairs, or furniture, you can keep them looking clean with a cream made from baking soda, talcum powder, and water. Slather it on the white areas and leave it for five to ten minutes. After that, proceed with cleaning using a sponge and warm water.

A small glass with coffee grounds placed in the refrigerator helps **eliminate bad odors**.

Eliminate moisture using coarse salt. Place two large cups of salt in a glass and place it on top of furniture in the upper areas of the house to eliminate moisture and prevent mold.

Cleaning is important, but that doesn't mean you need to give it lots of time or energy every day. Homes are made to be lived in, not to be spotless all the time. Nor do you need to run your dishwasher unless it's truly full. So, how should you schedule your cleaning routine to make sure you're doing enough for good hygiene and maintenance of your home, but without taking up too much of your time?

A good practice is to add daily cleaning into your regular routine. Setting a timer for twenty minutes a day and just cleaning up during that short time should help you keep your house clean without burning yourself out or letting chores stack up until they are overwhelming.

Some tasks, like washing dishes and sweeping floors, are usually done daily, while others may occur weekly or even less frequently. It's not a bad idea to create a schedule for these less frequent tasks. Things like washing window sills and checking fire alarm batteries do not need to be done all the time. Having a monthly calendar will allow you to set aside time for these chores. Don't forget things like oil changes, pulling out the

Christmas decorations, or prepping your yard for winter. There are a ton of detailed cleaning lists available online. There are even videos of normal people's routines, tips, and tricks readily available.

CHAPTER NINE:

FINANCES

BANKING

Thanks to technology, banking has become more convenient than ever. You may find that you hardly ever use cash to pay for things, opting for credit or debit cards instead. Some argue that only using these cards can be risky, because it's easy to lose track of how much you've spent when you can't see the cash in your hands. But that's not always the case if you learn how to manage your money wisely. If you are looking to open a bank account as a young adult, these are the things you should look for in a bank:

- No or minimum monthly fees
- No minimum balance required
- Reasonable fees on overdrafts

CHECKING VERSUS SAVINGS ACCOUNTS

You can have both types of accounts at the same time, and in fact doing so is encouraged, so that you can effectively save money that is separate from what you spend. The main difference between the two accounts is that the checking account is used for normal daily transactions. For example, when you use your debit card to pay for groceries, that money should come from your checking account. A savings account is primarily used for saving money over the longer term. A good habit is to make a detailed monthly budget to determine how much you need to spend each month on bills, entertainment, and other expenses, and then to leave that much in your checking account. Anything that's left over beyond what you plan to spend can be transferred into your savings account.

BUILDING CREDIT

Let's start with explaining what a credit score is.

Lenders—like banks—use credit scores to evaluate a person's ability to pay off their debts in a timely manner. In this way, credit scores determine one's eligibility for a loan and the interest rate they may be offered. The better (higher) your credit score is, the higher your chances of being granted a loan. If you are just starting to build your credit, sometimes it may be difficult to be approved for a credit card, since you don't have that strong credit history and high credit score yet. A good alternative may be to request a secured credit card. This type of card requires you to deposit an amount of money that you then cannot exceed each month.

Your credit score can be impacted by many factors, including:

- Payment history: whether or not you have always paid your debts on time
- Amount of money you owe: for example, how much of your monthly credit limit you've used. Normally using

less than 30% a month of your credit limit is preferred to build a good credit score

- Length of your credit history
- Amount of credit cards or loans you currently have

A common misunderstanding that credit card owners have, especially new ones, is the perception of a credit card as access to free money. A credit card represents a loan. At the moment you swipe your credit card, you are not using your own money—you are using your bank's money. Most credit cards have limits that are set by the bank depending on your income. Every month, you will be sent a bill for the money you've used through your credit card. Although having multiple credit cards can be useful to build credit, always make sure to pay off your debt either on time or before the due date. The best way to start with your credit card and to get used to it is to use it for small amounts, such as gas, and pay each expenditure off as soon as it appears on your statement. This way you will always pay off your debts ahead of time. This practice will have a great impact on your credit score.

HOW TO BUDGET

The best rule to follow when you are trying to save up money and still not miss out on fun things you want to do, is the 50/30/20 budget rule. This refers to your monthly expenses, which can be broken down as follows.

Spend 50% of your money each month on predictable, recurring needs and bills such as rent, utilities, food, wi-fi, car loans, phone payments, etc. Then, 30% of your money should go toward a combination of savings and paying off debt (if applicable), and 20% of your income should be spent on fun things like going to the movies, buying new items you want, or traveling on vacation.

Although it's not always possible, it is a good idea to try to spend no more than 30% of your income on housing (rent or mortgage). In other words, if your monthly income is $3,000, then you shouldn't pay more than $900 on your monthly rent or mortgage payment. This is the income percentage banks often use to calculate your mortgage eligibility.

A good way to calculate what you are spending is to look at your bank statements for the last three months. Figure out your average spending on rent, utilities, food, entertainment, clothes, and other expenses. This will give you a good idea of how much you need to set aside for each category and where you can improve when it comes to excessive spending.

TIPS FOR SAVING MONEY

Set Goals

When working toward your goals, it's a good idea to set small goals and build up to larger goals later. Most people aim to save at least 10% of their paychecks. For some people, though, this is just not possible. Even if you cannot save a consistent amount every month because of your living costs, you can still set saving rules for yourself. For example, maybe your goal might be to immediately pull your spending money from the bank in cash and save all of your change for a rainy day. Maybe you can put a dollar in a jar every time you spend on something frivolous like a fancy coffee or a trip to the movie theater. There are also a large variety of apps available to help you with saving and investing. Just make sure to do your research and make sure these are safe before creating an account.

Pay Your Bills and Yourself First

Before spending money on your wants, make sure you have your bills completely paid off and that you are also putting at least a little bit of your extra money aside before spending it. Even if you only have twenty dollars left, you should still section off a portion to put aside for emergencies and larger investments. It may seem like a tiny amount, but it will add up over time.

Wait Before Spending

If you want something, it's a good idea to wait three days before making the purchase. For example, when grocery shopping, make a list before you're at the store. If you find something you want from the store that wasn't on the list, add it to the list for your next trip instead of buying it immediately. This is a good habit to practice, as it will help curve impulsive spending over time. Many people end up wasting a lot of money on small purchases because they seem easier to justify than large ones. If you delay that gratification, you might find that you don't actually want many of the things you might have been ready to quickly buy on impulse.

Cook for Yourself

It's a good idea to cook the food you already have rather than dining out or ordering takeout. One way to ensure you don't waste food is to be realistic about what you will eat, how much time you have to spend on preparing meals, and what your common takeout temptations are.

For example, if you are prone to forgetting to eat until you feel extremely hungry or often don't have the time to cook large meals, it might be a good idea to stock up on snacks. Or maybe your issue is the time it takes to cook. You could chop your veggies and pre-cook certain ingredients so that the recipes you plan to make are easier and faster to finish. If you're regularly ordering a certain kind of takeout, consider making some similar dishes in advance for your freezer to heat up quickly when that takeout craving hits.

The worst thing would be to buy a bunch of food you will never eat. Be realistic about what you have the desire and time to prepare when it comes to your meals and snacks, and don't buy extras that might go to waste. If you are looking to change your habits, start small by adding one food or dish at a time into your routine. This will help decrease waste and keep you motivated.

Pack Your Lunch

Packing your lunch at home is a good idea to help prevent unnecessary and expensive meals out. If you are the type of person who forgets their lunch in the fridge or ends up waking up a little too late to prep, stock up on healthy snacks in your car, at your desk, and in your backpack, purse, or briefcase. Hunger can lower our tolerance to stress and increase the chances of "cheating" on ourselves. By keeping your body fueled, you make things easier for yourself and your wallet.

Grocery Shop Wisely

It's a good idea to make a list before buying groceries. Take stock of what you have in your fridge and pantry and plan meals that will use what is already available. You can also look in places like your local paper for various food deals and coupons. Another helpful idea is to write out a list of all of the meals you planned and shopped for. Keep it on your fridge, so you know what's available. That way, when your stock is running low, you still know what meals have enough ingredients to make. Last of all, make sure to eat before you shop. The last thing you want is to be hungry and suffering decision fatigue in the grocery store.

At the store, look through the shelves. Stores normally place the cheapest products on the bottom shelf, while the most expensive once are normally placed either on the top shelf or middle shelf, right at eye level, to catch your attention. Consider membership and loyalty cards for grocery stores if they tend to provide exclusive deals and coupons. Other good tips for not spending too much while grocery shopping are to compare prices between the different stores where you often go to buy your food, and to avoid buying foods that have been precooked or pre-cut, because the price of those prepared foods tends to be higher than the price of foods you need to prep yourself.

When shopping, don't be afraid to use a calculator; this will help you keep track of your spending. Before you head to the checkout, think about everything you put in your cart and ask yourself if you added anything that wasn't on the list that you don't strictly need, in which case you can put it back on the shelf.

Buy Secondhand

There are tons of options from secondhand goods. Thrift stores often have antique and used items salvaged from your local community. There are also online thrift stores and other websites that sell vintage goods. Social media sites often have groups and pages that are dedicated to locals selling their items, or even giving them away for free. Often there will be full "lots" available on these platforms for a flat rate. A "lot" might be an entire bag of clothes for a small price, for example. Another way to find good secondhand deals is to look for garage sales. These can be found by keeping an eye out as you drive through local neighborhoods. Another option is to gather with your friends and see if you all have anything you would like to trade. This can become a fun event with the right people and the right attitude.

Unsubscribe

Every once and a while, take the time to review your subscriptions and make sure you are using all of them. If you haven't used a monthly subscription in a month or more, unsubscribe. After all, it's usually pretty easy to re-subscribe to most things later on if you decide you want to use it after all.

Track Your Spending

As mentioned earlier, it's a good idea to keep an eye on your spending. Aside from averaging out the most recent three months, there are other techniques you can use to monitor your spending effectively. For example, only using cash will help make it easier to physically track how much you're spending and how often you're spending it. Another technique is to keep your receipts. In the past, people would keep a checkbook where they would write down the amounts they spent from their bank accounts. You can still find these, but they are much less common than they used to be. Instead, you can keep notes in your phone or maybe a small notebook that you keep on your person at all times. Even a small sheet of paper in your wallet can be helpful. Most banking websites now offer helpful budgeting tools and analyses of your spending patterns as well.

Skip Brand Names

Whenever possible, buy generic store brands rather than brand names. This can help you save for the brands that really matter to you. Consider what you are buying critically. The point of purchasing brand-name clothes is to buy higher quality that is longer lasting, so make sure that if you are spending the money on a brand name, you are actually buying items that are going to last for a long time, preventing you from having to replace them frequently. As far as food goes, most generic or store-brand items taste the same as brand-name items. You can always check the labels to see how ingredients compare or just take a gamble and experiment with cheaper brands. When it comes to attire, less can also be more. You don't need to be dressed head to toe in brand names to carry the same image as adorning a simple outfit with one branded item. Investing in a brand-name belt or a nice pair of shoes can dress up cheaper items of clothing without spending too much. If these things don't matter to you though, don't worry about it and only spend more if it's worth it.

Gas Up at the Right Time

Avoid filling up your car on the weekend or during the few days before major holidays, as the prices may increase during these days. The best time to get gas is usually early Monday or Thursday morning.

Create an Emergency Fund

Life is full of surprises and when you least expect it you may find yourself in an emergency situation. For example, you may find yourself without a job, perhaps because your company has gone out of business. Having an emergency fund available, in addition to the money you have set aside, will help you in a time of transition from one job to another.

Consider Investing

When people talk about investing, they often think of big expenses, such as buying a house, but this is not always the case. You can start by investing small amounts of money in stocks. There are even options to invest in penny stocks with tiny bits of money. If you use an app or website, be skeptical and complete thorough research before signing up for anything.

Save Receipts

Always keep your receipts. That way, if you find that an item is broken or doesn't work, you can always return it without having to keep something that doesn't work after spending money on it.

Scout for Discounts

Sometimes companies offer discounts if you decide to make package payments. For example, insurance companies apply discounts to customers who select to insure both their car and their home with the same company under one package.

Look for Side Hustles

Try to find some income other than your regular job that you enjoy doing and that does not cause you additional stress. For example, you could take a hobby of yours and make it marketable, such as designing websites, taking photographs, or playing piano.

CHAPTER TEN:
PERSONAL SKILLS

Especially in your young adult years, you should learn and practice these key personal (and interpersonal) skills, as they will help you throughout your daily life, even as you become busier and carry more responsibility.

Communication

It is so important to learn to communicate effectively with the people around you, including learning to listen well. Don't ignore what other people say, as you never know what might turn out to be a good life lesson for you. Learn to communicate with people who disagree with you or that you don't get along with; this way you will be more at ease around everyone.

Conflict Resolution

Learn how to resolve conflicts instead of holding grudges, as they will not bring you anything positive.

Develop Introspection

Learn to look inward, to observe your own flaws and work on what you want to improve about yourself. This will help you to build confidence and self-awareness, and is a sign of maturity.

Time Management

Learn to manage your time well, including allowing yourself enough time for each of the things that are important to you in life. Yes, you'll need time for work, but it's equally important to ensure you have enough time to relax, socialize, and do the activities that bring you joy and energy.

Patience

Learn to be patient, as things will not always go the way you want and expect.

Develop Balance

Learn to find a good balance between your professional life and your personal life.

Decision Making

Embrace the ability of making decisions efficiently and effectively, as this is something you'll do every single day.

Problem Solve

Learn to solve problems. Sometimes, it's easy to feel defeated by the situations we encounter in our lives. But never lose your strength—for every problem there is always a solution.

PLAN OUT
YOUR GOALS

Setting goals in your life is important, as they remind you of your purpose. Not only that, but setting goals helps you initiate new behaviors, gives you direction, and helps you identify what is important to you. To create an action plan for your goal:

Define your goal. Understand what you want to achieve and really think about what it will take to accomplish the goal. It's a good idea to keep a large, long-term goal, and then break that apart into smaller goals. For example, if your goal is to graduate with a 4.0 grade point average, then you will want to break that down into smaller milestones like receiving a 4.0 for each year, each semester, each term, and each class.

Make a list of all the tasks and steps you think you should take in order to achieve your goal. When completing this part of the process, it's a good idea to make each task as small as possible. This will help build a sense of self-sufficiency and confidence. If all of the steps are broken down into their smallest components, it makes them less intimidating to complete and helps keep the project manageable. For example, for receiving an A in a class, you would want to list out tasks such as finishing assignments as soon as they're assigned, never missing a lecture, planning out your study times, etc. This list could be broken down even further by breaking down each assignment into their smallest components. If you have to write an essay, you'll have to write an outline, a thesis, an introduction, body paragraphs, and a conclusion. You'll need to select your sources, read your sources, choose quotes, cite quotes, and complete a citations page. The goal here is to make each step as easy to accomplish as possible.

Set a reasonable deadline, so you don't lose track of your dream. It's a good idea to choose a specific date to finish each task by. It's okay to adjust the time frame as needed. After all, some things will take longer than we expect them to. With that said, it's a good idea to try your best to keep on schedule.

Prioritize the tasks on your list based on difficulty. Identify those tasks that are most critical and/or difficult and consider asking for help from someone who has experience doing something similar.

Celebrate milestones as you accomplish your goals. For completing a small task, maybe this means taking a short break. For receiving an "A" on a paper, maybe you go out to eat, buy a fancy coffee, or hang out with friends for a night. You can choose larger rewards for larger accomplishments. This helps keep you motivated and will also aid in preventing burnout. Self-care celebrations are really good choices when accomplishing smaller goals.

Identify the areas you have little knowledge about and do the necessary research until you feel confident you have all the knowledge and tools you need.

Monitor your progress, evaluate your progress, and improve where you can by learning from your mistakes.

NETWORKING AND BUILDING RELATIONSHIPS

Networking means sharing information and taking an active interest in new people. Thus, the goal is to try to reach outside of your comfort zone, which is probably represented by the people with whom you are closest and get along with best. The key to networking is to put yourself out there. Networking is all about the importance of building and maintaining new relationships. This doesn't mean you need to make lots of close friends, but rather try to make friendly or professional connections with people you can learn from, and who can learn from you.

Learning to establish human relationships that are peaceful, even in the context of a disagreement, is important because building this skill will help you to maintain calm in difficult situations and you will be more capable of managing your stress in a healthier way. Creating strong relationships, at work for example, helps improve collaboration, increasing both your own and collective productivity. It helps to exchange skills and knowledge that may one day be useful to you. Networking also improves creativity, since your mind is stimulated by outside thoughts and opinions. It can be easy to write people off quickly, especially if you don't get a good first impression, but this can be a mistake. Sometimes our strongest and most important friendships grow out of difficult beginnings, and these relationships can really help to improve our lives.

HANDLING STRESS

Some degree of stress is unavoidable; whether you are young or old, rich or poor, there is no such thing as a truly stress-free existence. At especially challenging times, it's important to know to deal with your stress in productive, healthy ways. When you find yourself under particular stress, follow these tips:

Reconsider your time and rebalance the time you spend on work versus the time you spend on yourself and what makes you happy. Remember that as a human being, your mind needs leisure in order to reset and stay in shape.

Create exercises for yourself that can help you divert your mind. For example, take a twenty-minute walk while you listen to some favorite music. It is a known fact that exercise—even gentle exercise—can provide a meaningful mood boost. It's even better if you have a friend to do this with!

Feed yourself well and limit your alcohol consumption. Some evidence suggests that alcohol consumption in the evening can increase feelings of sadness the next day, and it is well known that alcohol disrupts cognitive processes such as the ability to concentrate, solve problems, and make decisions. So while you may perceive temporary relief from alcohol consumption, in fact it is detrimental to your ability to solve the problems you may be facing.

Talk to supportive people. This can help to boost your confidence while providing care and comfort. If you don't have any friends or family members you feel comfortable talking to, you can often find online or in-person support groups focused on particular topics. There are also hotlines for a variety of subjects — not just for emergencies. You can find these phone numbers with a quick search online.

Carve out time to sleep. A lack of sleep and rest is linked to higher cortisol (stress) levels in the body. Your body needs sleep to function properly. During times of stress or illness, your body may require more sleep than during other times. If you are ever concerned you are getting too little or too much sleep, it's a good idea to talk to your doctor about it. Your doctor will help you to develop some possible solutions, such as monitoring your sleep schedule or checking for any underlying health conditions that might be impacting your sleep.

Take a vacation. If you can't afford the time and costs of traveling, you can create a vacation close to home or even at home. Sometimes taking a weekend to go camping in the next town over or maybe spending a couple days with a beloved family member is enough to reset your energy and perception.

It's important to step away from work and studies from time to time to relieve stress and prevent burnout.

Don't be afraid to seek help from professionals such as therapists when you are struggling. It's easier than ever to find helpful services. There are online apps to make therapy easier and many doctors will work on a sliding pay scale based on your income to help you afford treatment. Mental health is just as important as any other form of health care and should never be sacrificed. Just like you would go to a dentist to get your teeth checked if they were hurting, you should talk with your doctor about your mental health if you are noticing symptoms or struggling with your everyday life. Therapists can even help with things like goals and habit development for a healthier, happier lifestyle.

CHAPTER ELEVEN:
JOB INTERVIEWS

RESUMES AND COVER LETTERS

Having a good resume will help when you are trying to obtain a job. Your resume is the first impression that the recruiter or hiring manager will have about you, long before they meet you in person. When typing up a resume, many people fall into the trap of including way too much information—a full list of everything they've ever done and all of the skills they have. While showcasing important information about your background is the main role of a resume, remember that the document should be concise and to the point, containing only information that's relevant to the job you want. Here are a few tips for you to keep in mind when creating your next resume:

Keep your resume short and as direct as possible. Most professional resumes for young adults are only one page; that is typically enough to include all of your most relevant and important experiences.

Use a professional resume template if you aren't experienced in writing resumes from scratch. Developing all of the details of a resume template can be a big job—where to use italics or bold text? Should this be underlined, or not?—and also very time-consuming. Using a simple, professional template will save you all of that decision-making and allow you to focus on the content of what you're writing. Once you have a solid resume that is working well for you in terms of content, you may decide to update the format to something more personalized.

Use numbers. When talking about your experiences, make sure you include numbers wherever it makes sense to do so. Tell the reader how much, how many, and how often throughout the resume. Don't just say, "Planned events." Instead, say, "Planned 5 events, attracting 20+ people per event." Use the digits (5, 6) rather than writing out the words for the numbers (five, six).

Use professional and clear language to stand out, using strong action verbs to highlight your skills and accomplishments.

Write an effective cover letter to attach to your resume. You can find a lot of detailed guidance for developing a cover letter online or by talking to people in your network who have experience applying to jobs. Some tips you'll want to keep in mind are to address your letter to a specific person (for example, the recruiter or the supervisor), give specific examples that support your knowledge and skills, and use relevant action words to highlight what you've done.

MAKE A GOOD AND LASTING IMPRESSION

During a job interview, it's normal to feel anxious. You decided to apply for the job because you want the position! We all get a little nervous in that situation. But don't forget that the person interviewing you was also in your shoes once. Trying to keep your cool during a job interview will help you manage the situation in the best way possible. Here are some tips to keep in mind for your next job interview.

Prior to your interview:

- Conduct research about the organization.
- Practice a mock interview with a friend.
- Be prepared to discuss prior experiences.
- Plan the clothing you will wear.
- Plan your travel route to ensure you arrive on time.

Ask questions during your interview like:

- What skills are you looking for in a perfect candidate?
- What do you like about working at this company?
- How would you describe the company's work environment?
- Can you make an example of a typical day at work for this position?
- What are some of the most common challenges that this position faces?
- Is there something I can improve or learn before starting?
- What are some skills that are not considered essential but would be helpful for this role?
- Is there a dress code?

Choose what you will wear for your interview and when in doubt, go more formal. Every organization or company will have its own norms around typical dress depending on the work environment and company culture. It's hard to get a good feel for this until you actually work in that organization—so for an interview, opt for more formal rather than less formal attire. You can't go wrong with modest clothing, simple accessories, and a generally tidy appearance, though it's also okay to let your personality shine through.

Some additional quick tips for success:

- Bring a pen and a notebook to take notes.
- Arrive early at the appointment.
- Be respectful toward everyone you encounter during the interview process.
- Be honest when you are answering questions.

After your interview, it's a good idea to send a thank you note to each person who interviewed you, so that you can express your appreciation for their time and your continued interest in the position.

CHAPTER TWELVE:
BASIC ETIQUETTE

Good manners are the ability to behave appropriately in different social contexts. They are related to respect, kindness, and consideration toward others, though what is considered "good manners" varies tremendously by age, cultural background, location, and more. The tips below apply to general social etiquette in the business world in the United States, but may not be applicable to all locations, situations, or populations. Use your judgment and make your best effort to be respectful and polite to those you encounter, regardless of the context. If you are in a new place or with a group of people who are unfamiliar to you, observe their behavior carefully to pick up on their social norms. For example, do they shake hands when greeting, or kiss on the cheek?

In the United States, many (though not all) people are accustomed to the following behaviors and perceive them as polite:

- Make eye contact when greeting.
- Shake hands when meeting a person for the first time. You should shake hands firmly, but not too firmly, and without holding their hand too long or pulling it toward you.
- Assist your guests when they take off their coats in your home.
- Don't interrupt others when they speak; wait politely for your turn.

- Cover your mouth and nose when you have to sneeze or cough.
- Cover your mouth when you yawn.
- Be punctual and respect others' time. It's a good practice to set a watch fifteen minutes early, so that you are always on time.
- Always use the words "please" and "thank you" in your interactions, and especially when making requests.
- Introduce yourself and don't forget to introduce your friends to each other.
- Apologize if you run into someone.
- Never comment on a person's appearance, no matter what you think about it.
- When you borrow something from someone, always give it back and in a timely manner. A good rule is to never borrow something longer than three days unless you've specifically asked to keep it for a certain amount of time.

BASIC TABLE
ETTIQUETTE

It's wise to practice basic table etiquette at home before you need to know it for an event. You don't have to practice these things every day, but trying them out at the dinner table in the privacy of your home will help you feel confident when it is time to use these skills. Learning now will prepare you for when you need to attend more formal occasions.

When invited to lunch or dinner at someone else's home, try to resist the urge to add seasoning to your food. If you ask for lots of salt and pepper at the table, that may suggest to your host that you don't like the taste of the food they prepared.

Be mindful of your posture at the table. Your arms should be held along your side and only your hands should touch the tablecloth. Legs under the table should never be stretched or excessively relaxed. Ideally, everyone at the table should have a comfortable amount of room without being kicked or crowded on accident.

The napkin should be placed on the lap and brought close to the mouth only when necessary.

Bread should be broken with the hands and not cut with a knife.

Cell phones should never be used at the table.

TIPS FOR WORK ENVIRONMENTS

It's wise to practice work etiquette early and often. As we mentioned above, every work environment will have its own norms and practices, which you will start to figure out during your first weeks on the job. While the specific details will vary by employer, here are some quick tips that apply in most work situations:

Arrive on time. This is a sign of respect for your job, the organization, and your coworkers.

Wear appropriate attire. If you are in an office, business attire or business casual might be the standard. However, it would be rather odd to show up to a landscaping job wearing nice dress slacks. It's important to remember that different occupations require different clothing. If you are ever in doubt, you can always ask the manager or person in charge of hiring about dress codes when they call to set up an interview.

Choose practical footwear. If you have a job that requires you to spend a lot of time on your feet (for example, a server in a restaurant), make sure you wear something that will ensure your safety and comfort throughout your shift. Health codes require closed-toed shoes in commercial kitchens.

Electricians should be careful not to wear metal jewelry. It's also extremely important to have rubber soled boots to help decrease the chances of electric shock.

Business Attire can look many different ways, but in general you will want a collared blouse or shirt, nice dress slacks, and dress shoes. It's okay to wear a dress or skirt; however, special attention to the length and cut of the top is important. It's always a good idea to dress modestly. When it comes to women's shoes, keep in mind how much you'll be walking. Some people will wear comfortable shoes to and from work, and then choose to wear heels within the office to decrease the chances of blisters.

Construction and Landscaping workers should dress in layers to prepare for changes in weather conditions. Thick gloves and steel-toed boots are also a really good idea. In the case of outside work, bug spray, sunscreen, sunglasses, and a decent hat are not bad ideas to help protect against the elements.

Uniforms are assigned for many jobs. It's important to keep the standards set out by your manager. Sometimes this might even extend as far as to how you maintain your fingernails or style your hair.

Always knock before entering any office with the door closed or ajar, even that of a colleague who is waiting for you.

Keep your workstation neat and organized. This is not just for the benefit of other people. You are more likely to remain focused and efficient if the areas you are responsible for are tidy. This is especially important for any and all jobs relating to food or in jobs that might be dangerous like construction work.

Keep your personal life personal. This is for your protection and reputation. Hopefully your work environment is fun and uplifting; however, at times you may encounter coworkers that don't have your best interest at heart. If you remain professional and keep your personal life out of the workplace, there are less opportunities for gossip or conflict. This is also important when it comes to protecting your work/life balance. If someone asks you to cover one of their shifts, and you say no, you don't have to tell them why. If you want to spend your day off in your pajamas eating ice cream instead of covering someone else's shift, it is perfectly fine to do so.

Be diplomatic when resolving conflict. It's always a good idea to follow the "chain of command" when it comes to handling disputes. This starts with you and your coworker. Whatever the issue is, try your best to remain unemotional and professional about the problem. If you and the person are unable to come to a good resolution, then take it up to the next level of leadership. This may be a shift manager or team leader. It's important not to skip people in the chain of command. For example, don't go straight to your manager without talking to your coworker first, or jump right to the head of your department before attempting to get help from your manager. Whenever possible, try to keep on good terms with your coworkers.

CONCLUSION

As scary as this transitional time in life can be, it can also be very exciting. Always remember that we learn the most by making mistakes, so don't be afraid to get out there, practice your independence, and try new things. This book has provided tips on everyday situations that may often seem simple but can actually be quite complex, especially if you are new to them. Don't be afraid to ask for help when you need it. Asking for help never makes you weak; on the contrary, it will strengthen you as a human and as an adult. Learn to live life with a proper balance of seriousness but also lightheartedness, responsibility but with a touch of fun.

Printed in Great Britain
by Amazon

53274241R00079